The Human Sciences

Volume III

Carkhuff and the Possibilities Science

Bernard G. Berenson, Ph.D.

POSSIBILITIES
PHENOMENA

PROBABILITIES
MOMENTS

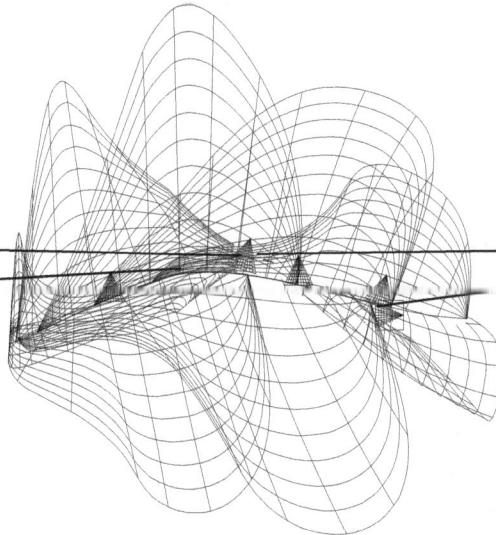

PROBABILITIES
MOMENTS

Published by: HRD Press, Inc.
                     22 Amherst Road
                     Amherst, MA 01002
                     800-822-2801 (U.S. and Canada)
                     413-253-3488
                     413-253-3490 (fax)

ISBN 978-1-61014-400-1

Editorial services by Robert W. Carkhuff
Graphics and production by Jean S. Miller
Cover design by Eileen Klockars
Promotion by Swift Global Media

The Human Sciences

Volume III

Carkhuff and the Possibilities Science

Contents

About the Author

Bernard G. Berenson, Ph.D., was a long-time co-processor with Carkhuff. He was director of the first Center for Human Resource Development at American International College. In this capacity, he served as co-director of the Springfield Project for Community Resource Development.

Berenson was author of *The Possibilities Mind* (2001) and co-author of numerous books with Carkhuff, including especially *The New Science of Possibilities* and *The Science of Freedom.*

Dedication

To Bernard G. Berenson,
my long-time co-processor and co-creator.

Conversations with Bernie and Friends

A Eulogy to Bernard G. Berenson, Ph.D.

Bernie came from the outer spaces of the universes. He came to save our place called earth and the earthling people who resided there.

His mission was to civilize us: To save us from ourselves.

A Conversation with Einstein

Before he came, he had conversations with Einstein. Bernie called him Ike after his wartime leader.

"What are the rules of engagement?" he asked.

Ike replied, "I've worked out equations for the probabilities in the 5 percent of the universes that we know anything about!"

Bernie gulped, "What about the other 95 percent?"

Ike equivocated, "The Black Holes and Dark Matter are not understood yet!"

Ike added, "Better check with God. He has the whole caboodle of knowledge. I'm the Probabilities Part. He's the Possibilities Whole!"

Bernie liked Ike, but he definitely wanted the whole caboodle.

A Conversation with God

So Bernie went to God and repeated his question: "What are the rules?"

God: "When I got Moses to come up the mountain, we created hundreds of rules."

Bernie: "So what happened to them?"

God: "We cut it down to ten—didn't have enough tablets."

Bernie: "How does that work?"

God: "To tell the truth, it doesn't! People can't remember them. No memory span!"

Bernie: "So what are you going to do, God?"

God: "I'm cutting it down to more manageable numbers."

Bernie: "So what are the rules?"

God: "There is only one rule: relate."

Bernie: "I've come a long way. You've got to give me more than that."

God: "If you want to be a helper, you have to relate."

Bernie: "Just keep relating?"

God: "Just keep relating to everything and relate everything to everything else."

Bernie liked God. God called him by his familiar name, "Bud." (What Bernie didn't know is that God called all men "Bud" or "Buddy.")

Bernie was resolved: "Just keep relating to everything and relate everything to everything else!"

In Communion with the Community

Before Bernie descended upon the community, he reflected upon an inspiring idea: God had named his only son "Yeshua," meaning "Helper" in Hebrew, translating to "Jesus" in English. It gave him confidence that God had put him on the right track for helping.

When he entered the community, he began relating to everyone and everything. He related everyone to everyone else. He related everything to everything else.

He related them to each other: individuals to organizations (homes, schools, colleges, governance, businesses).

He related different communities to each other: underclass to working class to middle class; white to black to brown.

He related everyone to things that they wanted to do with their lives.

He related organizations to achieve their most productive functions.

He related communities to become their most prosperous forms.

He helped everything real to become an ideal form of itself.

For those who couldn't help themselves, he would train them; for those who couldn't learn, he would empower them; for those who couldn't even start, he would do it for them.

For Bernie, the whole community became a growing center.

People never committed crimes again. Welfare recipients never indulged in any forms of entitlement!

People became college educated. Workers had their positions elevated. They became idea generators and skilled innovators.

Some people became entrepreneurial sources of the community's prosperity. All people were committed to participating in the community's governance.

They loved their communities as if they were alive.

In relating, Bernie discovered there was indeed a rule, only one rule, God's rule: "Do unto others as you would have them do unto you."

They related to each other as if God were in the other person. And He was!

In Communion with the Universe

Bernie also related ideas to ideas. He took note of the scientists attempting to relate one side of their equations to the other side of their equations. He related to the equations as if they were alive.

He had an insight into relating itself. Just as no two people were alike, so were no two cells in the universe the same.

He discovered his Principle of Unequality. God never replicated anything in the world. All phenomena were uniquely differentiated. Even sides of equations!

Bernie followed God's reasoning: It is only if they are different that they can truly relate! It is our differences that empower us to relate synergistically.

The same cells are the same cells! Period! They cannot relate.

Now Bernie understood God's basic principle: Cellular interdependency cannot occur without cellular differentiation.

The Principle of Unequality became the foundation for us, his colleagues in R&D working to develop virtual representations of the processing of the universes. In so doing, we are empowered to generate mutual generativity with humans.

In perspective, Bernie came from the outer spaces of the universes in order to improve our planet, our galaxy, our universe.

He fulfilled his God-given mission to relate to us and save us.

In the process, he related to the universes themselves, maybe even to save them from themselves with an understanding of Unequality.

So there it is! He returns to the universes from which he came.

I see him now, with his ideas reverberating through the universes, secure in the knowledge that, like matter, ideas cannot be destroyed.

Cascading through the ages, he takes his place among the sages.

Bernie lives forever with the universes that he has enlightened with an understanding of Unequality.

R.R.C.

Book I:
The Science of Change

Chapter 1
Paradigm Change ━━━━━━━━

Over our adult lifetimes, Robert R. Carkhuff and I have processed inter-dependently to service all forms of human endeavors and needs. Mostly, we sought solutions to current human predicaments by changing the dimensions of the predicaments—requirements of conditions, component inputs, transforming processes, function outputs. Usually, we generated new and more effective paradigms for elevating the growth and development of the people and their endeavors.

In so processing, we were empowered to conceptualize and operationalize "The New Science of Possibilities (11)" and contradistinguish it from The Science of Probabilities (see Table 1):

Table 1.
Levels of Possibilities Science

5. **Freeing**

4. **Empowering**

3. **Relating**

2. **Prediction**

1. **Describing**

As may be viewed, the **Relating** and **Empowering** functions of possibilities were built upon **Describing** and **Predicting** functions of probabilities and dedicated to the ultimate possibilities function, **Freeing** or **Releasing** the potential of all phenomena.

All of which brings us to the measurement of achievement in its feedback to the systems that it shapes. In the **Probabilities Sciences, Parametric Measurement** assumes the normal distribution of all dimensions of all phenomena (see Figure 1):

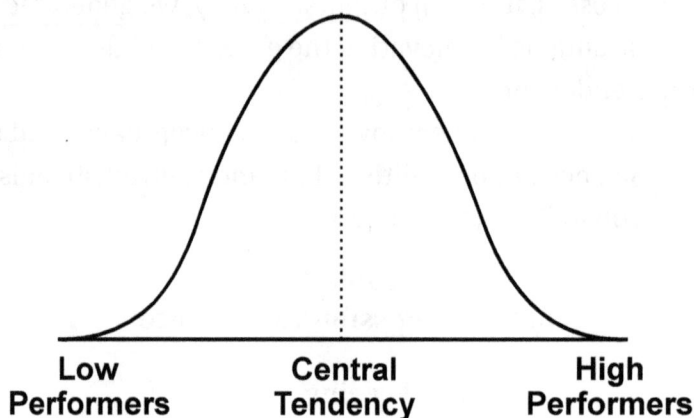

Figure 1. The Normal Distribution of Parametric Measurement

As may be viewed, the data are equally distributed around the central tendency, all of which makes the phenomena and their performances describable and predictable.

Carkhuff's greatest contribution is The Generativity Paradigm that empowers traditional sciences with "Human Intentionality." In so doing, he introduces a whole new paradigm of Paradigmetric Measurement (9, 10). Just like the operational definition of an objective, "Paradigmetrics" measure the dimensions utilized to construct the new paradigm. Thus, the curve moves in the direction of the high performers defined by the new paradigm (see Figure 2).

Paradigm Change

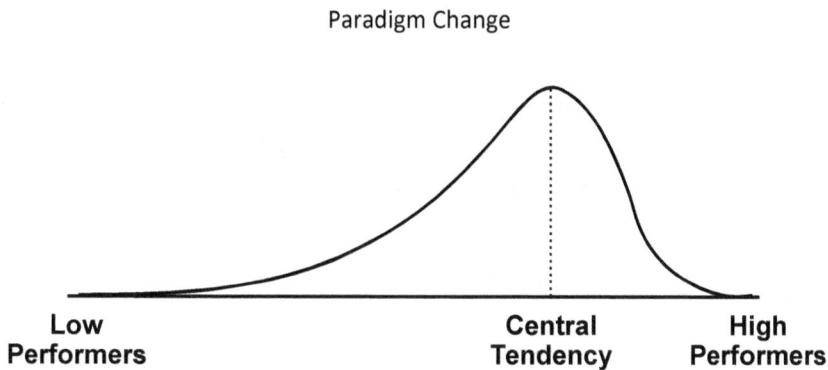

Figure 2. The Directionful Movement of Paradigmetric Measurement

As may be viewed, the central tendency is moving toward the high performers while leaving a static tail of data behind them. This empowers the phenomena involved to improve performance with the freedom from the "norms" of restrictive measurement.

We may view the formation of a **New Paradigm.** In Figure 3, data represent the movement from the **Old Paradigm** to the New Paradigm (9, 10):

OLD

NEW

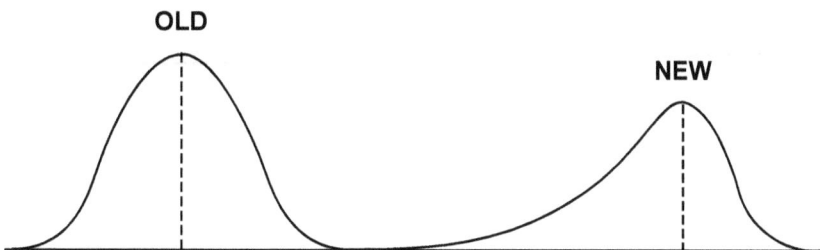

Figure 3. The Formation of a New Paradigm

For example, the New Paradigm may move away from controlling functions to freeing functions; from linear content to multidimensional content; from independent processing to interdependent processing. One produces "Probabilities in a Static Society." The other generates "Possibilities in a Changing Society."

In transition, **Possibilities Science** generates new and more effective paradigms for elevating measurement, including **The Generativity Sciences** and their **Paradigmetric Measurement. Paradigm Change** is what human growth and civilized human endeavors are all about. **Paradigm Change is Carkhuff's Possibilities Mission!**

In introducing Dr. Robert R. Carkhuff's body of work, I must first represent myself as his long-time co-processor who has been impacted in much the same ways in our study of science: by behaviorism, by phenomenology, by ideation. I, myself, have published my conclusions concerning Carkhuff's enduring scientific contributions.

Carkhuff's career in science has been generated interdependently, developmentally, and cumulatively through all areas of human endeavor: individual, organizational, community, cultural, economic. However, rising above these cutting-edge applications are Carkhuff's contributions to "The Science of Science."

This is the story of Paradigm Change.

Chapter 2
Scientific Influences ——————

Carkhuff credits major historical influences upon his direction and development as the sources of his generativity (see Figure 4).

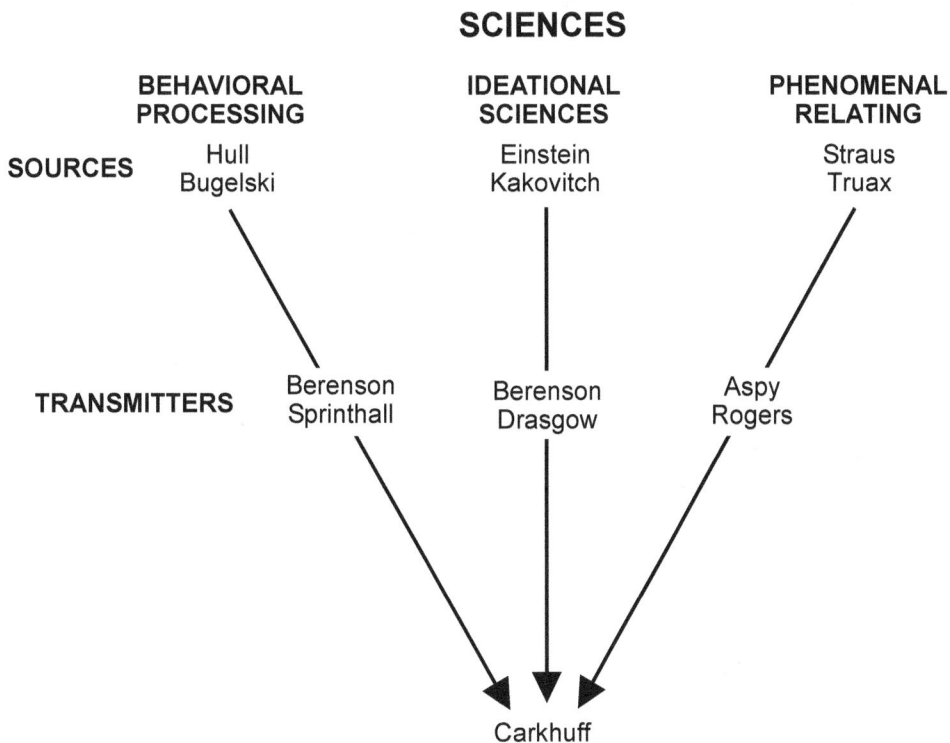

SCIENCES

	BEHAVIORAL PROCESSING	IDEATIONAL SCIENCES	PHENOMENAL RELATING
SOURCES	Hull Bugelski	Einstein Kakovitch	Straus Truax
TRANSMITTERS	Berenson Sprinthall	Berenson Drasgow	Aspy Rogers

Carkhuff

Figure 4. Scientific Influences on Carkhuff

The first and enduring scientific influence is that of Clark L. Hull and B. R. Bugelski—**Behaviorism.** The second influence was the **Phenomenalism** of Erwin Straus and Charles B. Truax. The third influence was the **Ideation** of Albert Einstein and Tom Kakovitch.

Hull, Bugelski, and Behaviorism

First of all, B. Richard Bugelski, his mentor in graduate training at SUNY, Buffalo, introduced Carkhuff to conditioning and learning (3, 4). Specifically, Carkhuff was introduced to the **drive theory** of Clark L. Hull, Bugelski's own mentor (18, 19, 20):

$$sEr = sHr*D$$

- **sEr** = excitatory potential or the likelihood that the organism will produce a response to the stimulus

- **sHr** = habit strength, which is derived from previous conditioning

- **D** = drive strength, determined by conditions such as deprivation

It is Hull's attempt to formulate a universal equation for explaining behavior that stimulated Carkhuff's lifelong mission of generating The Science of All Scientific Processing.

Secondly, these scholars transmitted **S–O–R** learning theory emphasizing intervening variables (unobservable behaviors) in the form of an organismic repository of **S–R** conditioning responses. In so doing, they extended the work of both John Watson (31) and Ivan Pavlov (22), founding fathers of psychology, from peripheral Stimulus–Response (**S–R**) events to central Organismic (**S–O–R**) learning phenomena.

It is this **S–O–R** platform upon which Carkhuff created his Generative Processing (**P**) paradigm (**S–P–R**) which has become the foundation for all of our higher-order Phenomenal Processing Systems (**S–PP–R**) (2).

As may be observed in Figure 5, each level of processing is nested or housed in higher-order levels of processing:

- S–R in S–O–R or Discriminate Learning Systems
- S–O–R in S–P–R or Generative Processing Systems
- S–P–R in S–OP–R or Organizational Processing Systems
- S–OP–R in S–PP–R or Phenomenal Processing Systems

In differentiating itself from **S–R Conditioning** and **S–O–R Learning,** this **Paradigmetric Processing Scale** reflects the evolving nature of the substance of processing (9, 10). Here it should be noted that Carkhuff was well grounded in **Parametric Measurement** by Bugelski (3, 4) and Sprinthall (27, 28).

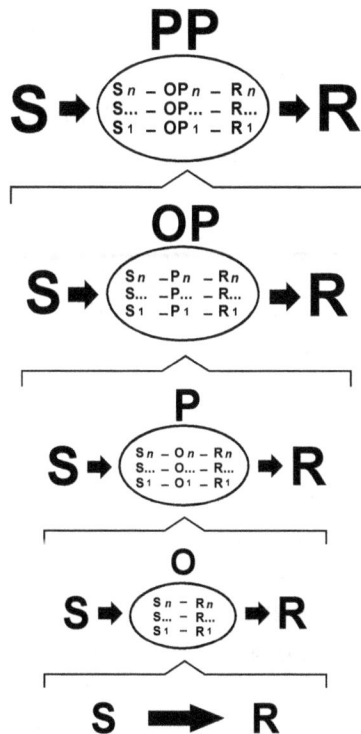

Figure 5. Levels of Phenomenal Processing

9

Straus, Truax, and Phenomenalism

Upon graduation, Carkhuff obtained an NIH Postdoctoral Research Fellowship to the Universities of Wisconsin and Kentucky to work with Truax (30), Straus (29), and Rogers (23, 24, 25).

Straus's research in phenomenalism began with the hominid's assumption of the upright posture. From this basic assumption, humankind went on to develop its general intelligence and social relating core. The basic assumption of phenomenalism became the basic assumption of all science: "All science begins with the sensory experience of the scientist."

In turn, Rogers's contributions to client-centered treatment began with his assumption of "the actualizing tendency," the life-force motivation residing in every life form. Nourishing and freeing these life forces in distressed people was the function of Rogers's non-directive therapy. He contradistinguished dark forces, which must be analyzed and controlled.

The enduring contributions of Exceptionalism (23, 24, 25) has been due to the initial attempts by Truax at operationally defining the constructs involved (30): **TPC = C + E + R.**

- **TPC = Therapeutic Personality Change** as measured by client **Self-Exploration** and reality-based outcome measurements defined by Truax and Carkhuff (30)

- **C = Congruence** or therapist **Genuineness** as adopted from Carl Whitaker's *Technique of Family Therapy* (31) and refined by Truax and Carkhuff (30)

- **E = Empathy** or therapist **Understanding** adopted from the Neo-Freudians and measured by the accuracy of reflections refined by Truax and Carkhuff (30)

- **R = Respect** adopted from Rogers's **Unconditional Positive Regard** and refined by Truax and Carkhuff (30)

Building upon this platform, Carkhuff and associates went on to factor analyze and operationally define the core ingredients of all helping and human relationships (2, 7, 8, 9):

$$(R \leftrightarrow I) \rightarrow LLW$$

- **R** = **Responsiveness** incorporating empathic understanding modified by differential regard
- **I** = **Initiative** incorporating operational definitions of goals and concrete programs to achieve them
- **LLW** = **Living, Learning,** and **Working** indices of concrete achievements

To sum, the synergistic relationship between **Responding (R)** and **Initiating (I)** affects all human endeavors **(LLW)**. In extensive research of more than 160,000 helpees, Carkhuff established the pre-potency of these relationship factors in all living, learning, and working endeavors. Succinctly, when helpers are functioning at high levels of both **R** and **I**, they are successful in 95% of the **LLW** outcomes (11).

Again, Carkhuff's sustaining contribution to these learning experiences was generating a scale for phenomenal relating (9) (see Figure 6):

LEVELS	OPERATIONS

5. GROWING
(Interdependent)

$$R''' \rightarrow \boxed{\text{Interdependent Relating}} \rightarrow R'''$$

4. MERGING
(Interpersonal)

$$R'''$$
Merge
$$R' \quad \text{Get} \quad \text{Give} \quad R''$$

3. GIVING
(Independent)

$$R' \quad \text{Get} \quad \text{Give} \quad R''$$

2. GETTING
(Dependent)

$$R' \quad \text{Get}$$

1. GOALING
(Orienting)

$$R'$$

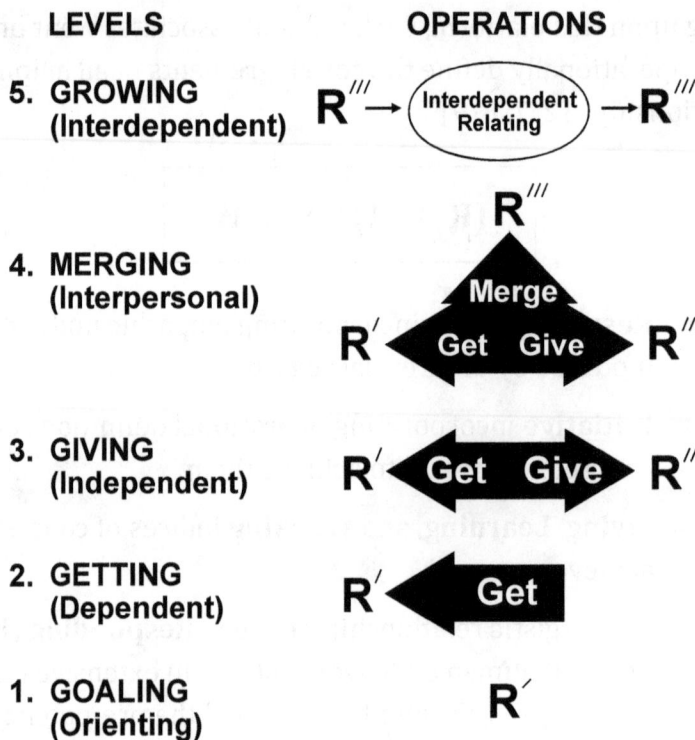

Figure 6. Levels of Phenomenal Relating

As may be noted, each phase is nested in the higher-order phases:

- Goaling in Getting
- Getting in Giving
- Getting and Giving in Merging
- Merging in Growing

In differentiating itself from the responsive level of phenomenalism, this Paradigmetric Relating Scale reflects the evolving nature of the substance of relating (9, 10).

Einstein, Kakovitch, and Ideation

The third and most powerful scientific influence upon Carkhuff was the Ideational Theorizing of Albert Einstein and Tom Kakovitch.

While Einstein did not generate Possibilities Science, he did express his hopefulness:

> *I am convinced that someone will eventually come up with a theory whose objects, connected by laws, are not probabilities...*
>
> — Albert Einstein (Letter to Born)

Fortunately, we were the beneficiaries of his stimulation and inspiration (11).

Einstein did not so much establish a theory of thinking as he did establish its values and model its practices. Universally regarded as the "Father of Modern Physics," he recommended a "single, consistent theory" as the explanation of all observations. He sought the factored elegance of "what was really going on, underneath it all." For example, in his cosmology, he applied The General Theory of Relativity to model the structure of the universe as a whole.

To be sure, Einstein's work also provided a platform for The Hypothetical–Deductive Modeling of later thinkers such as Hull. In this regard, Einstein recommended the following:

> *Scientific work proceeds best from an examination of physical reality and a search for underlying axioms, with consistent explanations that apply in all instances and avoid contradicting each other.*

For his "Thought Experiments," we regard Einstein as the model for generating ideation. Inductively, this means observable foundations for probability statements with highly-leveraged explanations or paradigms that visualize projections. The use of the a priori principles or models in "Experiments in the Mind" has become a standard model for modern thinking in all scientific areas.

In short, Einstein recommended theories that were "elegant" in their nature: the minimum of constructs with a maximum of explanation. Although he had a lifetime of difficulty with mathematics, he summarized the most powerfully leveraged formula in scientific history in simple, elegant terms:

$$e = mc^2$$

In turn, Kakovitch, recognizing the diminishing effects of Force Fields within a continuously expanding universe, offered proofs for the existence of a pre-potent **Fifth Force** (21): the constancy of temperature and radiation in continuously changing universes.

Drasgow, in turn, influenced by this great scientist, sought Non-Parametric ways to represent the measurement of ideation. In so doing, he rejected the dominant statistical assumptions of the normal distribution required by Parametric Measurement. Drasgow sought functionality in the sophisticated Non-Parametric statistics of Sidney Siegel and John Tukey (26).

All of these scientists converge their scientific missions upon the explanation of the unknown. For his part, Carkhuff emphasized the deductive flow of model-building: from elegant theory to possibilities statements to testable hypotheses in the unremitting search for new and more powerful phenomena (9, 10, 11).

Once again, Carkhuff's take-away from his mentoring experiences was a scale for ideational phenomenal information (9) (see Figure 7):

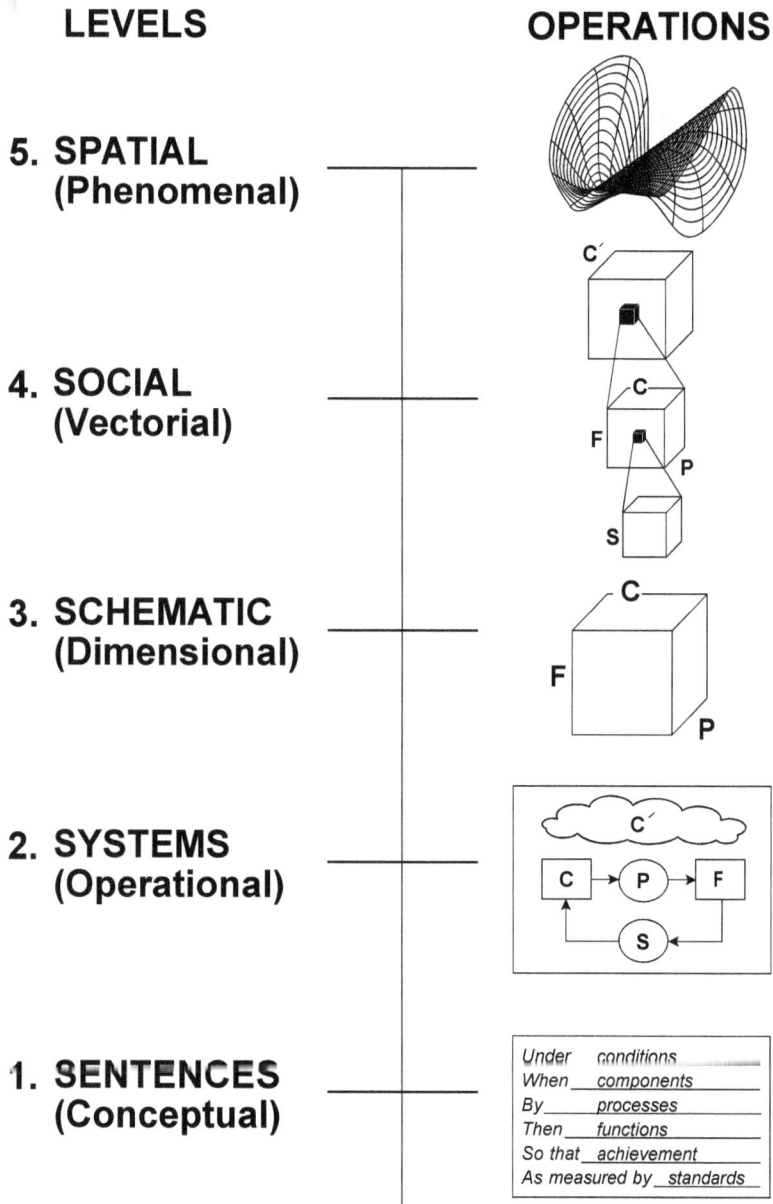

Figure 7. Levels of Phenomenal Information

As may be viewed, each level of information is nested in higher-order information:

- Conceptual sentences in Operational systems
- Operational systems in Dimensional schematics
- Dimensional schematics in Vectorial schematics
- Vectorial schematics in Phenomenal schematics

This Paradigmetric Ideational Scale incorporates the vectorial and phenomenal levels of information modeled by Einstein. To be sure, it represents the evolving nature of the substance of information (9, 10).

Chapter 3
Scientific Generativity ——————

Perhaps the major contribution of Hullian Behaviorism to Carkhuff was Hull's **Hypothetical–Deductive Modeling System.** This method generated precise definitions and axioms that enabled the efficient testing of hypotheses and the formulation of theories. Ultimately, Hull believed that behavior was a set of interactions between individuals and their environments.

Hypothetical–Deductive Modeling

Hypothetical–Deductive Modeling became a foundation upon which Carkhuff built his systematic methods of Inductive Probabilities Model-Building and Deductive Possibilities Testing (10) (see Figure 8).

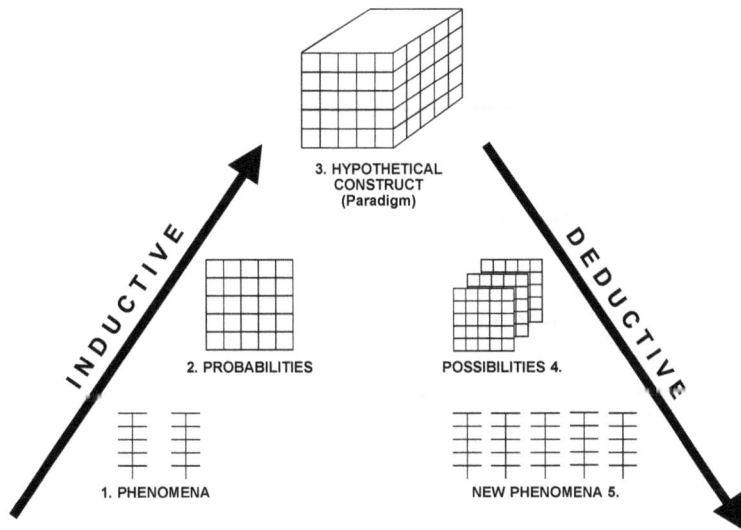

3. HYPOTHETICAL
CONSTRUCT
(Paradigm)

INDUCTIVE

DEDUCTIVE

2. PROBABILITIES

POSSIBILITIES 4.

1. PHENOMENA

NEW PHENOMENA 5.

Figure 8. Building and Testing Hypothetical Constructs

As may be viewed, hypothetical constructs are built inductively as follows:

1. **Phenomena:** The observations of stable phenomena are factored and scaled in related dimensions.

2. **Probabilities:** The dimensions are formulated in Probabilities Statements (historically laws) that are related in operational systems and matrices.

3. **Hypothetical Construct:** The probabilities dimensions are then related in Hypothetical Constructs or Paradigms (historically theories) that are related multidimensionally in schematics and models.

In turn, these Hypothetical Constructs are the source of systematic Deductive Hypothesis Testing:

4. **Possibilities:** The Possibilities Statements are deduced from the hypothetical constructs occurring under differing phenomenal conditions (historically theorems) that are formulated socially as vectorial relationships.

5. **New Phenomena:** The hypotheses are deduced from the Possibilities Statements and tested empirically for achievement under differing phenomenal conditions resulting in new phenomena.

The Hypothetical–Deductive Modeling and Testing continues with the generation of new phenomena in replacement of the old phenomena: observations, probabilities, constructs, possibilities, hypotheses. Together, they culminate in the generation of New Hypothetical–Deductive Modeling.

Carkhuff has summarized the operations in building Hypothetical–Deductive Constructs in a Paradigmetric Scale (see Table 2):

Table 2.
Building Hypothetical Constructs Paradigmetrically

Levels	Operations
5	Relating the Vectors Phenomenally (Spatial and Curvilinear)
4	Relating the Models Vectorially (Social–Schematics)
3	Relating the Systems Dimensionally (Schematics and Models)
2	Relating the Factors Operationally (Systems and Matrices)
1	Discriminating the Substance Conceptually (Factors and Scales)

These are the **Paradigmetric Rules** he follows for generating new ideation.

Generating Ideation

Carkhuff has illustrated Hypothetical–Deductive Modeling in his Paradigmetric Scale of New Capital Development or NCD Models (11) (see Figure 9). We may learn much from Carkhuff's scientific approach to this most difficult of constructs, New Capital Development or NCD by focusing upon the operations of one level of NCR—MCD or Marketplace Capital Development.

As may be viewed, NCD is modeled deductively:

5. MCD or Marketplace Positioning Functions
4. OCD or Organizational Alignment Functions
3. HCD or Human Processing Functions
2. ICD or Information Modeling Functions
1. mCD or Mechanical Tooling Functions

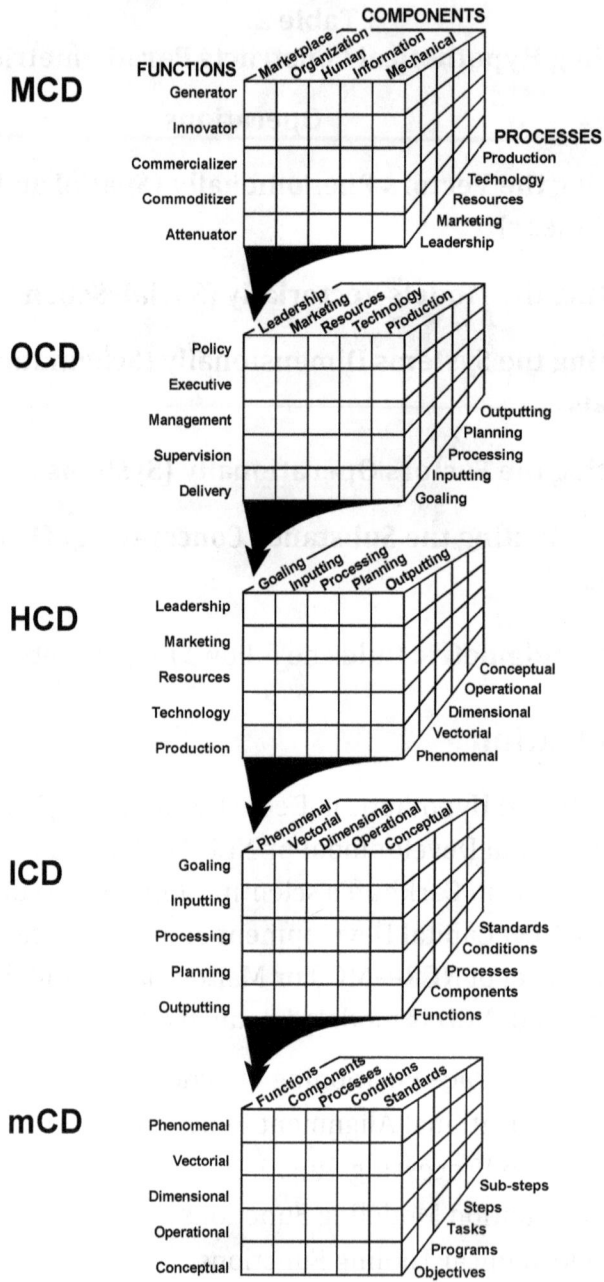

Figure 9. Deductive Modeling in New Capital Development

There are other rules that govern Hypothetical–Deductive Model-Building:

- All lower-order systems are nested or housed deductively in higher-order systems:

$$MCD > OCD > HCD > ICD > mCD$$

- All lower-order systems are coded deductively by higher-order systems:

$$MCD > OCD > HCD > ICD > mCD$$

- All lower-order systems may be rotated inductively to become higher-order systems:

$$mCD > ICD > HCD > OCD > MCD$$

This Hypothetical–Deductive Model generates all of the processes that are required to accomplish marketplace missions:

- Marketplace Positioning
- Organizational Alignment
- Human Processing
- Information Modeling
- Mechanical Tooling

Moreover, these models enable the efficient testing of hypotheses and the effective building of New Hypothetical–Deductive Models.

Operations of Marketplace Positioning

We define Marketplace Positioning as the relationship of organizational or corporate capabilities to marketplace requirements within the lifecycle of the market. Corporate capabilities may be defined in terms of corporate technologies—the methodologies that organizations have incorporated into their business, whether or not these methodologies are for sale directly. In turn, marketplace requirements are defined by customers. Marketplace requirements are the capital or most important products, services, solutions, and relationships — the ones that customers deem necessary to ensure their own successful performance in the marketplace. The market's lifecycle is defined and measured by levels of growth in gross and profitability and in market penetration. Our positioning in the marketplace is defined by the relationship between our corporate technologies and the "capital" requirements of our customers within the market lifecycle.

Equipped with the information above, we can develop an operational model for representing marketplace requirements. We label our model "MCD," or "Marketplace Capital Development." Building it involves four general steps:

1. Scaling the functions or requirements of marketplace positioning

2. Scaling the components or capabilities that are representative of the technologies available to service marketplace requirements

3. Scaling the market lifecycle of these functional requirements and corporate technologies

4. Representing the interaction of these elements of **MCD** in a three-dimensional model

We manage our Marketplace-Positioning responsibilities by using our scaled **MCD** positioning information. We cross our requirements and capabilities scales to develop matrices of Marketplace-Positioning information. By bringing these into interaction with the third scale, the market lifecycle scale, we develop a three-dimensional model of Marketplace-Positioning information. These scales, matrices, and models provide us with useful material for analyzing our current and future Marketplace Positioning.

Scaling Marketplace Requirements

We begin modeling our marketplace positioning by scaling the requirements of the marketplace. A useful generic description of the functions or requirements of the marketplace is found in the analysis of **New Capital Development** or **NCD** economic factors shown in Figure 10.

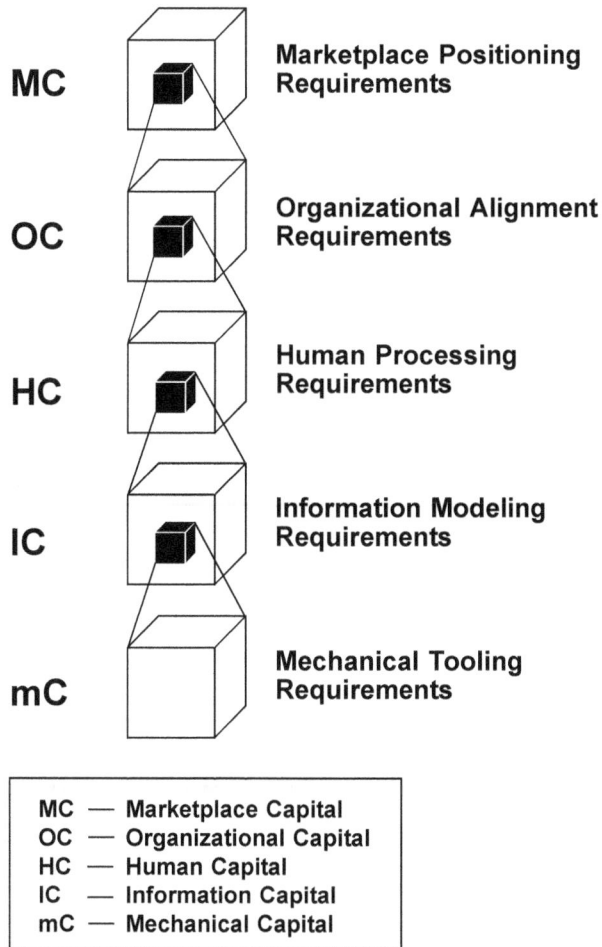

MC — Marketplace Positioning Requirements

OC — Organizational Alignment Requirements

HC — Human Processing Requirements

IC — Information Modeling Requirements

mC — Mechanical Tooling Requirements

MC — Marketplace Capital
OC — Organizational Capital
HC — Human Capital
IC — Information Capital
mC — Mechanical Capital

Figure 10. Marketplace Requirements in New Capital Development

This figure allows us to see the marketplace requirements as **NCD** requirements; it also shows us how the requirements are related. We may note the following:

- Mechanical Capital (mC) Requirements are driven by Information Capital (IC) Requirements.

- Information Capital (IC) Requirements are driven by Human Capital (HC) Requirements.

- Human Capital (HC) Requirements are driven by Organizational Capital (OC) Requirements.

- Organizational Capital (OC) Requirements are driven by Marketplace Capital (MC) Requirements.

Our analyses of the Marketplace Requirements begin with the evolving need for New Capital Development or **NCD** in all forms.

This table of Marketplace Requirements is a map-in to initial marketplace requirements. Further analyses of each type of **NCD** provide a clearer description of the specific market requirements that we need to measure. Each set of **NCD** Requirements is a subset of this generic scale of **NCD** Marketplace Requirements. As we learn more about how to model and manage each of these **NCD** sources of wealth, we discover many useful *nested* market requirements—scales to aid us in our marketplace-positioning responsibilities.

If we want to stay in business, we have no choice but to respond to Marketplace Requirements. Once we have defined those requirements, the only remaining question is "How will we respond to meet the requirements?" Many organizations will respond, and a few exemplary ones— Possibilities Organizations— will even exceed the responses required and actually generate new requirements based upon their relationships with customer organizations.

Scaling Corporate Capacities

Corporate Capacities are needed to satisfy the **NCD** Requirements of the marketplace. Corporate Capacities are defined as technologies that are used to fulfill Market Requirements (see Figure 11). We define Corporate Capacities by **NCD** Technologies to address **NCD** Requirements.

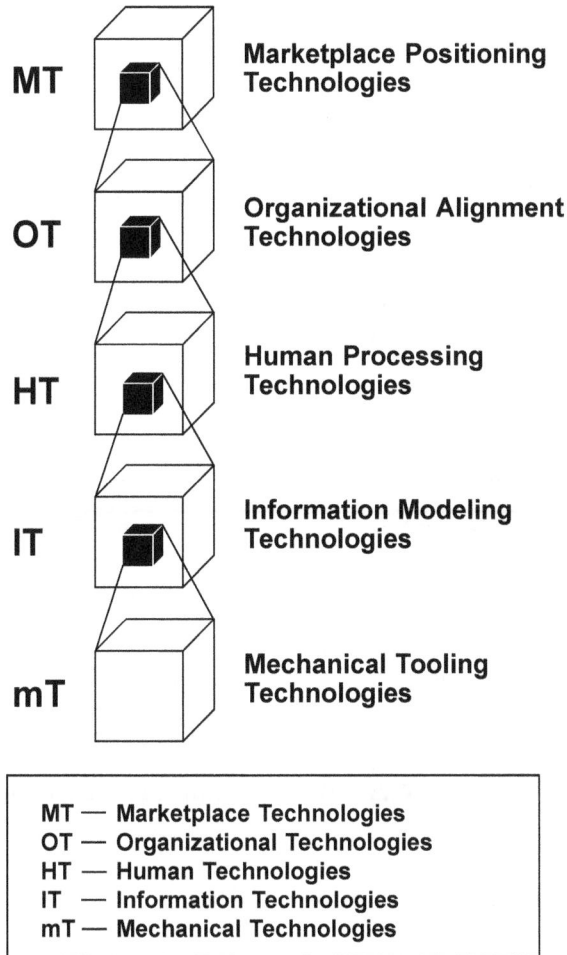

MT — Marketplace Positioning Technologies

OT — Organizational Alignment Technologies

HT — Human Processing Technologies

IT — Information Modeling Technologies

mT — Mechanical Tooling Technologies

MT — Marketplace Technologies
OT — Organizational Technologies
HT — Human Technologies
IT — Information Technologies
mT — Mechanical Technologies

**Figure 11. Corporate Capacities in
New Capital Development Technologies**

Scaling the Market Lifecycle

The ability of corporate capacities to achieve marketplace requirements is dependent upon placement in the **Market Life Cycle**—the so-called "**GICCA Curve**" (see Figure 12).

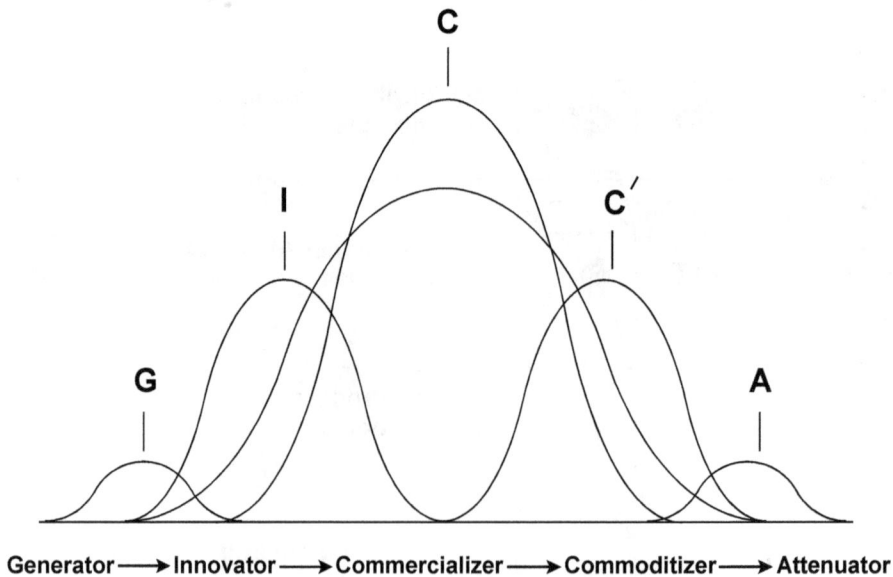

Generator ⟶ Innovator ⟶ Commercializer ⟶ Commoditizer ⟶ Attenuator

Figure 12. Phases of the Market Lifecycle

The bulk of the market falls with the commercializers. Here are the sources of the Market Lifecycle:

- **Generators (G)** create the market with breakthroughs.
- **Innovators (I)** transfer the breakthroughs to customer contexts.
- **Commercializers (C)** commercialize the market by expanding customer uses.
- **Commoditizers (C')** continue the market by producing more for less.
- **Attenuators (A)** exploit the market in its decline and to its end.

This Market Lifecycle applies to the evolution of *all technological break-throughs* and *all* products, services, and solutions. We may represent the lifecycle in a simple scale, as shown in Table 3.

Table 3. Market Lifecycle

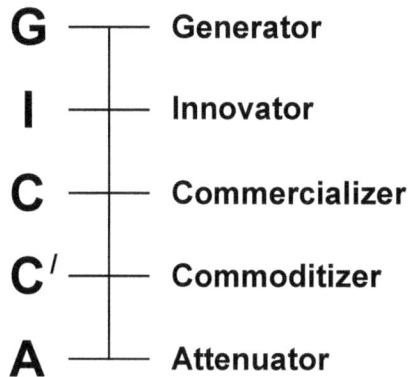

G	**Generator**
I	**Innovator**
C	**Commercializer**
C'	**Commoditizer**
A	**Attenuator**

The prepotent issue for twenty-first-century corporate leaders is this: *How do we empower and accelerate our corporations to become drivers, rather than riders, in the marketplace?* The short answer is simple: Inter-dependency — within, between, and among Generators, Innovators, and Commercializers. The implementation of this relationship releases the power of the marketplace to the policy of the corporation.

In the Market Lifecycle, the Generators are initially outside the adoption curve and their products are brought into the curve by the contextual transfers of the Innovators. The Generators are interdependently related to their substance and its environment, and usually only tangentially related to the market. The Innovators, in turn, are oriented to the application of breakthroughs in the context of customer concerns.

The gaps between both processes and products of Generators and Innovators are large, while those between Innovators and Commercializers are enormous. In the final analysis, such gaps within the marketplace can be bridged only by Commercializers who are themselves interdependently related to the market's visions of its own needs. The Commercializers' functions are the most complex of all: to be interdependent with customers and technologies. Commoditizers take over when the Commercializers have lost their relationships with either the marketplace or their technologies, or both. Attenuation soon follows.

In Marketplace Capital Development, we position our organizations by forming interdependent relationships across the phases of the Market Lifecycle. To ensure that their corporations are dedicated to growth, the Commercializers relate interdependently with Generators (who are able to create markets), and with Innovators (who are able to make transfers and applications that initiate the market's movement).

Scaling the Organizational Functions

With organizational positioning calculated, the company is now ready to operationally define its functions (see Figure 13):

- **Policy**: Positioning in the market lifecycle
- **Executive**: Architecture to align resources
- **Management**: Systems to implement alignment
- **Supervision**: Objectives to accomplish objectives
- **Delivery**: Tasks to produce products and services

As may be noted, each level of the organization is nested and therefore encoded by the requirements of higher levels. We are now prepared to learn about **The Science of Science.**

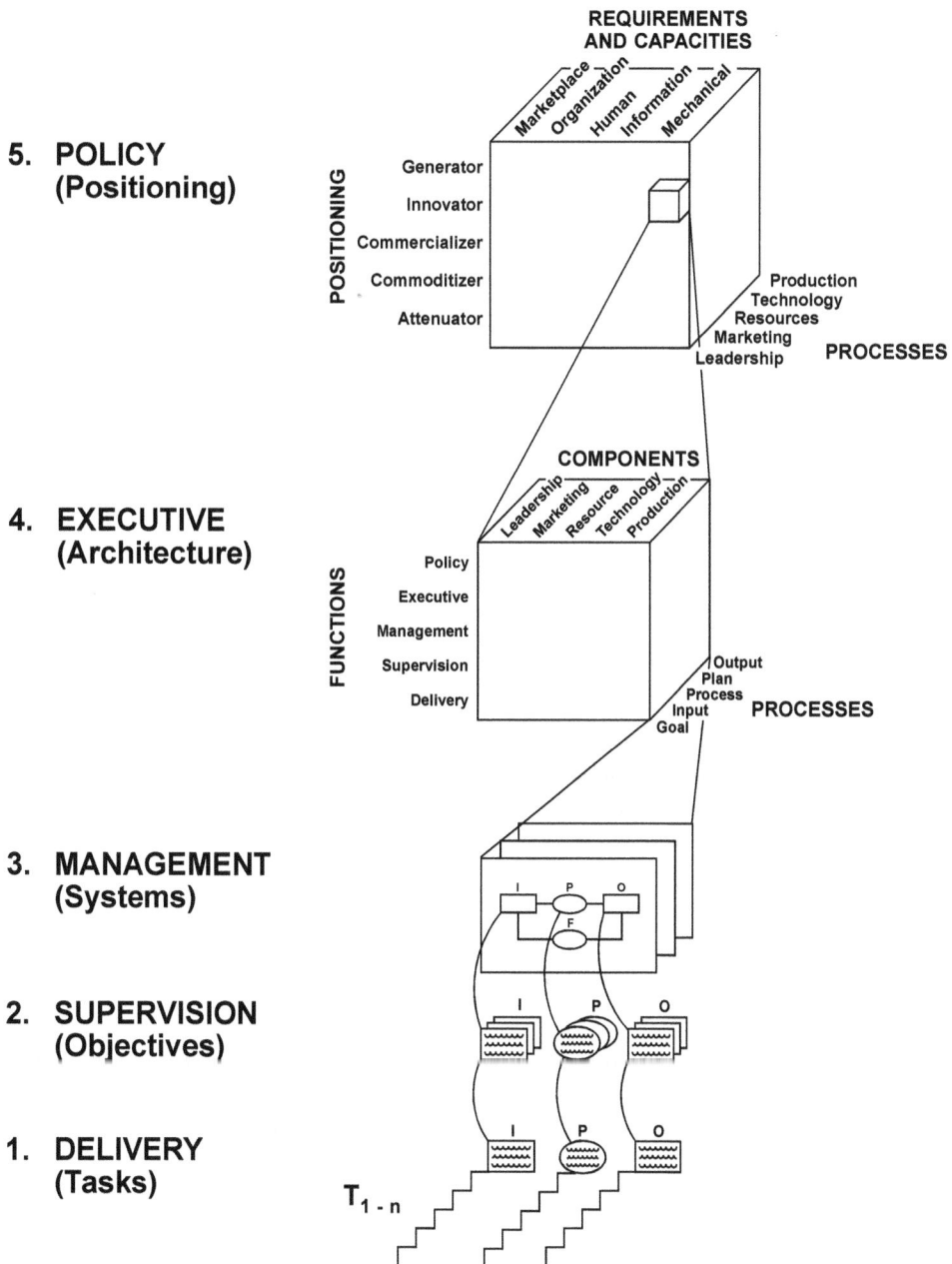

Figure 13. Levels of Organization

Book II:
The Science of Science

Chapter 4
The Science of Science ————————

In one sense, Carkhuff had his science delivered to him on a "golden platter." Hullian Behaviorism, Strausian Phenomenalism, and Einsteinian Ideation. The measurements were straightforward and operationally defined:

- **Parametric Measurement** by Bugelski (3, 4) and Sprinthall (27, 28).
- **Empirical Measurement** by Drasgow and Truax (30),
- **Non-Parametric Measurement** by Siegel and Tukey (26).

In another sense, Carkhuff differentiated himself from thousands of other learners by his General Intelligence. Always guided by psychological meaning, he knew what to do with the gifts of conceptual knowledge:

- Operationally, factoring the phenomena and scaling their dimensions
- Dimensionally, relating the scales in models
- Vectorially, relating the models socially
- Phenomenally, relating the vectors spatially

Paradigmetric Modeling

Empowered by Hypothetical–Deductive Model-Building, Carkhuff constructs his models "paradigmetrically" (9):

Level 1. Discriminating Factors Conceptually
Level 2. Relating Factors Operationally
Level 3. Relating Systems Dimensionally
Level 4. Relating Models Vectorially
Level 5. Relating Vectors Phenomenally

As may be noted, the levels are built systematically to nesting vectorial models in phenomenal contexts. Again, these are the **Paradigmetric Rules** that he follows for generating new ideation.

The secrets to **Paradigmetric Modeling** are systematically building the operations of the paradigm by nesting, encoding, and rotating the dimensions involved. Just as we define objectives by the operations needed to achieve them, so do we define paradigms by the systems needed to architect them. Just as we measure our levels of achievement of objectives by the operations we accomplished, so do we measure the achievement of paradigms by the systems.

Carkhuff views **Paradigmetric Scaling** through the eyes of the phenomena themselves. Not only is this scaling defined by the generativity of creative thinking, but also by the generativity of generational differences.

The Paradigmetric Scales are not defined by probabilistic scaling—nominal, ordinal, interval, and so on. They are differentiated by the measurable processing power of generational differences.

These differences are exponential. Indeed, they may be experienced as infinite from the time and space of their platform of origin.

For Carkhuff, the differences are exemplified by the differences between ourselves and the generations "sandwiching" us. In a healthy and growing civilization, we will be exponentially more powerful in processing than the generation before us. In turn, the generation following us will be exponentially more powerful than we are.

Carkhuff projects that the next generation of empowered Possibilities Scientists will generate their own phenomenal, changeable, operational, and therefore measurable worlds. In so doing, they will culminate visions of infinite scalability and universal applicability to which Carkhuff adds the simple edict of civilization: **"Pass it on!"**

So what might Carkhuff do with his newly scaled levels of science? He follows the rules of ideation for Paradigmetric Measurement—deductively relating the scales in models dedicated to organizational processing (see Figure 14):

- Marketplace-Driven Functions
- Organizational Processing Components
- Human-Processing Processes

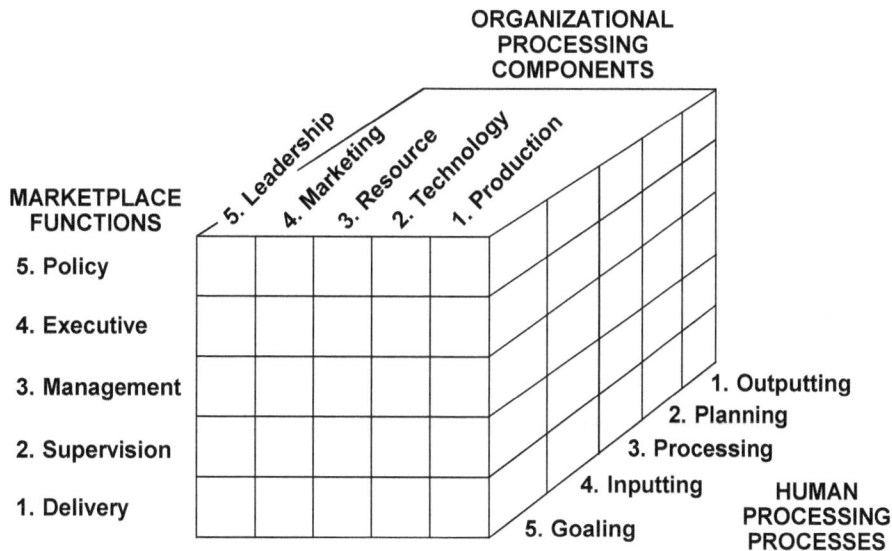

Figure 14. Organizational Processing Model (Deductive)

Translated verbally, this phenomenal integration means the following:

Marketplace-driven policy functions are accomplished by leadership-driven organizational processing components empowered by goal-driven human processing systems.

In other words, we can accomplish our organizational policies at the highest levels by leadership enabled by individual generativity.

We may see the benefits of Paradigmetric Modeling in sharp relief by focusing on any one cell in the Paradigmetric Model. For example, the 5-5-5 cell yields the following operational definition of mission:

Organizational positioning in the marketplace is achieved by leadership-driven organizational processing enabled by goal-driven generativity.

This is the processing that must take place in a healthy policy-making cell that sets the direction of the organization in operation.

The advancement of science is found in the generation of elevated levels of Paradigmetric ideation, as is the advancement of civilization found in the generation of possibilities! In Carkhuff's terms: "Science is ideation!"

The Science of Generativity

The fundamental assumptions of Probabilities Science revolve around the principle of variability: variability is the range of deviations from some central tendency such as a mean, median, or mode; the central tendency becomes the standard, and we usually seek to narrow our tolerances around the standard.

The fundamental assumptions of Possibilities Science revolve around the principle of changeability: changeability is found in the "error variance" of probabilities measurement. It is accounted for by the ongoing rotation of operations in the universe; these rotations enable the continuous interdependent processing of all phenomena.

Thus, The Probabilities Scientist seeks to continue some artificial ideal and to order everything and everyone in a way that conforms to that ideal. The science derives from this controlling function:

- We **describe** phenomenal operations.
- We **predict** phenomenal operations.
- We **control** phenomenal operations.

This controlling function has served humankind in the production of a spiraling array of goods and services. However, it does not align itself with the inherent changeability of all natural phenomena.

The Possibilities Scientist, while not abandoning Probabilities Science, seeks to align with the natural and changing operations and rhythms of phenomena. Accordingly, the science culminates in a releasing or freeing function:

- We **relate** to phenomenal operations in order to understand their potential.

- We **empower** phenomenal operations in order to enhance their potential.

- We **free** phenomenal operations so they may actualize their potential.

This freeing function will serve humankind in the fulfillment of its human and environmental potential to actualize our destinies.

The central principle here is changeability. Changeability defines the standards by which we operationally define all phenomena:

Changeability is the key to this operational definition.

Whereas variability seeks to fix phenomena in a static state, changeability seeks to align with, first, naturalistic operations and, second, empowering interventionistic effects upon operations. Its view is inclusive, admitting variability as simply another instance of the changeable. Variability itself, though, is exclusive, and eliminates all concepts of changeability.

These two contrasting principles shape the core of two very different sciences. Probabilities Science, which relies on variability, is highly artificial in origin, contributed by humankind's need to order and control its universe. This science fixes its data sources in two-dimensional matrices of rows and columns. It analyzes its data in statistics concerning the deviation of phenomena from derived central tendencies. In so doing, it loses much of the measuring of its original data through so-called "error variance." In this context, chaos and even relativity are misinterpretations.

Possibilities Science comes to us fashioned by observations of Nature's operations:

- Phenomenal processing
- Inequality of processing
- Nested processing
- Genetic encoding of processing
- Rotating of processing systems

Together, these operations make up the continuous interdependent processing systems that define changeability. If we are continuously and interdependently processing, then we are continuously changing.

Changeability is the prepotent construct. It generates an infinite array of spiraling standards and serves as the driving function for variability. It empowers us to do *the right things,* while variability enables us to do *things right.* On occasion, we may even dedicate changeability to variability and the eternal task of narrowing variability around static standards. For example, statistical process control is dedicated to narrowing tolerances in mechanical tooling for fine and fragile functions.

In short, changeability is the engine of possibilities—the energy source of Nature's intelligence. It is a free seminal generator, certainly not something to be partitioned like variance. The artificiality of the latter may be employed to support a temporary fad-like commercial product or idea, or even scientific content; yet, all processing phenomena are ever, in truth, changeability companions.

Chapter 5
Generating Possibilities ─────────

Carkhuff does not believe in any one monolithic processing system: "In a civilized society and a sane community, there are people at every level who are processing interdependently to discharge their functions."

The Assumptions of Possibilities

The human efforts to scientifically process phenomenal experience may be termed "Possibilities Science." Possibilities Science enables us to release or to free phenomena. The operative word here is *free:* the freedom of all phenomena, including human, is a function of the phenomenal processing systems; we relate to phenomena in order to comprehend their processing potential; we intervene to empower phenomena and thereby enhance their processing potential; we free phenomena in order to release their processing possibilities within God's universes of phenomenal possibilities.

The assumptions of Possibilities Science enable us to generate this freedom (1, 9). The first of these assumptions is the **multidimensionality of phenomena.** Multidimensionality is assumed in the dimensions of the phenomenal processing systems: driving conditions, component inputs, transforming processes, function outputs, measurable standards (9, 10) (see Figure 15). In other words, phenomena, whatever their form, are inherently multidimensional.

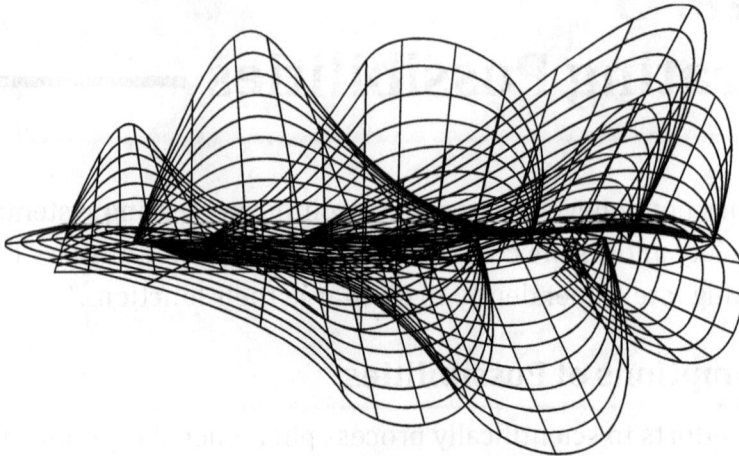

Figure 15. The Assumptions of Possibilities

The second of these Possibilities Science assumptions is the **interdependence of phenomenal vectors in the universe.** Interdependence is assumed in vectorial terms. This does not mean mutual dependency, but partnered processing for potentially mutual benefits; partnered processing between scientists and phenomena; partnered, virtual processing between phenomena and phenomena. In other words, the relationships between interdependent vectors are interactive and synergistic: each grows as the other grows.

The third of these assumptions of Possibilities Science is the **asymmetry of the phenomenal curves.** When we work with the data excluded from probabilities analyses (which assume independent factors and normal distributions), we find that asymmetrical curves define the essence of the phenomena. We thus assume asymmetrical models of the changing nature of phenomena: there is no baseline from which the phenomena vary, only infinite and asymmetrical changeability.

The fourth assumption of Possibilities Science is the **dynamic and continuous changeability of these interdependent vectors.** Changeability is assumed in terms of 360 degrees of global freedom or diversity: due to the continuous expansion of the changeability of *all* vectors, the changeability of *any* vector is continuous. In other words, only the continuously changing phenomena are enduring: the only constancy is change.

The culminating assumption of Possibilities Science is the source of changeability: **process-centricity, the continuous processing of all phenomenal dimensions.** Process-centricity is the generating principle of all possibilities science: the multidimensional, interdependent, asymmetrical, and changeable processing of all dimensions. In this context, not only the dimensions but also the processing systems themselves are continuously changing.

Generating Expanded Possibilities

The implications of these assumptions of Possibilities Science are profound. Generativity expands global possibilities of continuously changing, interdependent, and asymmetrical multidimensional phenomenal vectors. These phenomenal possibilities are due to the processing ability to align with the phenomena in their naturalistic form. We may regard these phenomenal possibilities as process-centric in a potentially infinite web of networks reflective of Nature's universes of changing phenomena.

We may view possibilities and probabilities phenomena in perspective in Figure 16. As can be seen, probabilities phenomena occupy a small window of opportunity in space and time. Indeed, we may think of them as Probabilities Spaces rather than as phenomena in themselves. They occur within infinite possibilities phenomena. This is the essence of Possibilities Science. probabilities spaces occurring within the context of infinite possibilities; possibilities phenomena ensuring that we have accurate phenomenal perspectives of probabilities.

**POSSIBILITIES
PHENOMENA**

**PROBABILITIES
MOMENTS**   **PROBABILITIES
MOMENTS**

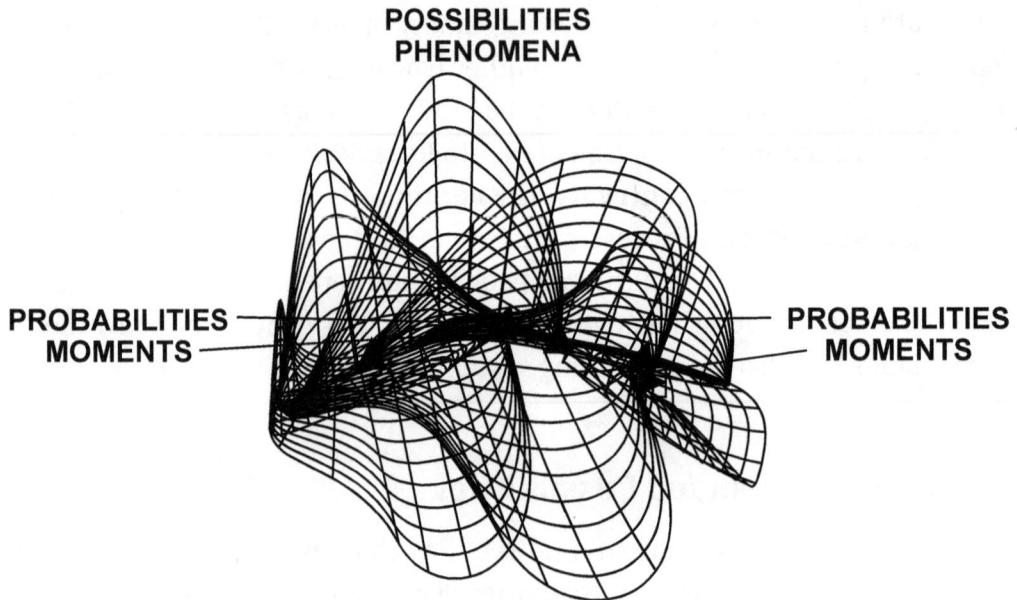

**Figure 16. Probabilities Phenomena in a
Possibilities Phenomenal Context**

When we produce products and services of any nature—whether they involve people, data, or things—we employ possibilities to drive probabilities: possibilities ensure that we are *doing the right thing for our purposes.* We employ probabilities to produce our products: probabilities ensure that *we are doing things right.*

In turn, our possibilities design incorporates probabilities. Surely, we may employ probabilities, such as our knowledge of *best practices* in specific areas, to empower scientists to generate possibilities designs. In this instance, our probabilities empowerment enables our possibilities design.

To introduce possibilities models representing phenomenal possibilities, we may employ probabilities imagery: linearity, right angles, singular curvilinear tracks, and the like. However, the asymmetrical nature of phenomenal possibilities provides the framework for empowering probabilities moments: whatever the nature of phenomenal processing, the phenomena will reconfigure asymmetrically. *Thus, we can now freely employ Paradigmetric Models to provide perspectives for static models:* whatever the nature of the phenomena, they will change continuously—birthing, growing, dying, rebirthing—to discover and rediscover their own changeable forms.

We also emphasize information models of all phenomena, doing so because we can understand them most readily. That is the nature of Possibilities Science. If information lives, then we can generate Paradigmetric Models for everything. In this context, all science is applied science: **everything lives!** For Carkhuff: **"Information lives forever."**

While these sciences and the phenomena they generate are interdependently and synergistically related, the power of one dominates the contributions of the other: possibilities are expanded, elevated, infinite; probabilities are narrowed, reduced, infinitesimal. Possibilities have been God's province. Probabilities have been, until now, humankind's province.

Although humans can be justly proud of their probabilities contributions, those contributions are infinitesimal in relation to our infinite phenomenal universes. The entire history of civilization, for example, has revolved around limited resources such as energy: discovering, extracting, refining finite resources of fossil fuels—coal and shale, oil and gas. Indeed, in the twentieth century, we fought two great world wars primarily over energy, killing more than 100 million people and destroying the lives of hundreds of millions of others.

Now, drawing from the generativity of the fictional *Star Trek,* we may employ ion-driven, solar electric propulsion systems to thrust our spacecrafts into the heavens. Someday, burning fossil fuels will simply be a memory trace for civilization: a *probabilities moment.* What kind of a civilization will we create when we learn to align, enhance, and release the infinite phenomenal resources of God's multiple universes?

No, the describing, predicting, and controlling functions of Probabilities Science are not going to define and actualize our brave, new, and prosperous world! Neither are the parametric assumptions, planning paradigms, and statistical process controls!

Yes, the relating, empowering, and freeing functions of Possibilities Science are going to generate and innovate our continuously growing and changing human and phenomenal destinies! Our unfettered, Paradigmatic Assumptions and process-centricity are going to release the power of the universes to literally and physically make everything out of nothing but our brainpower and our Paradigmetric Models: our precious science of possibilities that drives our technologies of probabilities.

Clearly, in Possibilities Science, we serve the freeing functions. The power of Possibilities Science is found in the interdependent processing of matured scientists with the phenomena they are addressing. The interdependent processors discern and apply the powerful forces guiding our universes: multidimensionality, interdependence, asymmetry, changeability. Both processor and phenomena mature!

Generating Phenomenal Possibilities

Possibilities Science is both source and force; content and processing; means and ends of all possibilities. Only our egos and their illusion of independence prevent us from understanding the interdependent nature of the universe.

We may represent these phenomenal possibilities symbolically by continuously changing, multidimensional, interdependently related, and asymmetrical curvilinear dimensions (see Figure 17). Indeed, just as phenomenal possibilities are changing, they are also expanding: quantitatively in the direction of the force of their vectors; qualitatively in their increasingly inclusive power to create space and time. They are like all-powerful changeable crystals, constantly exploding in curvilinear space with new and interdependently related, multidimensional systems: each yields the infinite possibilities of the changeable wholeness of our multiple universes.

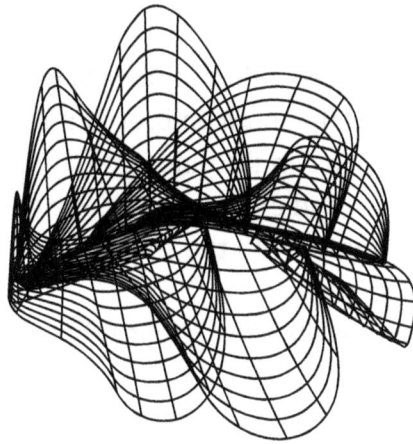

Figure 17. Generating Phenomenal Possibilities

As these universes of possibilities expand, they generate Probabilities Moments: opportunities upon which Probabilities Science may capitalize. As these universes of possibilities contract, they *become* probabilities phenomena. In this context, with the perspective of temporal and spatial distance, they collapse their multidimensionality in singularity (see Figure 18). However, Nature, having no tolerance for singularity, will again explode to generate new and changeable and expanding phenomena.

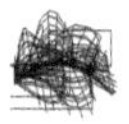

Figure 18. Singularity

In summary, the culminating implications of Probabilities and Possibilities Sciences contrast vividly: infinitesimal to infinity! Given the constancy of linear, independent, and symmetrical phenomena, Probabilities Science is planning-centric and narrowing. In contrast, given the changeability of multidimensional, interdependent, and generative phenomena, Possibilities Science is process-centric and expanding. Only continuous processing can align, empower, and free the perpetual motion of changing phenomena.

The fundamental principles of Possibilities Science thus empower us to generate infinite possibilities that both embrace and resolve the apparent conflicts of relativity and chaos: multidimensionality, interdependence, asymmetrical curvilinearity, and changeability. We can neither explore our universes nor penetrate infinity with the simplicity of the equations of Probabilities Science: $x = y.$

Indeed, the models of Possibilities Science that have been represented are highly initiative and, as such, have limitations even as they move inexorably toward discovering the nature of Nature and its phenomena: multidimensional, interdependent, curvilinear asymmetrical, changeable: $x \neq y.$ For Carkhuff, this is "Humankind's Work"!

The phenomenal models, in turn, require a higher level of alignment through relating; of enhancing phenomenal potential through empowerment; of freeing phenomena to discover their own changing destinies. They are therefore experiential, evolving, and unifying; they express the changing basic fabric of developmental merging toward singularity and the resulting explosion of infinite possibilities. For Carkhuff, this is "God's Work"!

Chapter 6
The Possibilities Mind ———————

For 50 years, I have labored in the possibilities vineyard with Bob Carkhuff. Only it was a labor of love for:

- The phenomenal beauty of alignment with Nature
- The truth of "factored" knowledge
- The excellence of deductive applications

During this time, we have had many "truths" revealed to us, for example:

- The "interchangeable responses" of interpersonal communication that led to the early development of Human Capital or HC

- The transformation of "data points" into information that defined the early stages of Information Capital or IC

- The synergistic relationship between Human and Information Capital Development that operationalized Human Generativity as HCD ↔ ICD

Together, they define the ingredients of The New Human Sciences generated by Carkhuff.

In my relationship with Carkhuff, I have had the special privilege of an unequal and interdependent processing relationship, where we are each, alternately, mentor and learner. Together, we formulated The New Science of Possibilities (9), an answer to Einstein's most fervent plea.

Stimulated by his expanded experience of phenomenalism with Erwin Straus (29), Carkhuff has generated the Human Relations Movement and defined the models for Human Capital Development.

Elevated by The Hypothetical–Deductive Models of Hull, Carkhuff has probed all levels of Information Representation and operationalized Information Capital Development.

Freed by the courageous "Thought Experiments" of Einstein, Carkhuff has defined Human Generativity as the synergistic interaction of Human and Information Capital: each grows as the other grows.

In summary, Carkhuff has defined The Science of Human Generativity and its Paradigmetric Measurement. This Human Science processes interdependently with all phenomena of Nature, thus measuring the ingredients of the paradigms of all phenomena being studied.

Following is The Carkhuff Generativity Processing Paradigm in his own words.

Generativity Processing Systems

Paraphrasing Newton, it is often said by scientists of scientists that we build our sciences upon the brainpower of **GIANTS.** I have done so. I have built The Science of Change in interdependent processing with GIANTS—in reality where possible, in "virtuality" where not. Mostly, I have built The Science of Phenomenal Change "with" representatives of these GIANTS—Berenson being my most powerful interdependent processing partner in my lifetime in science.

Basic Tools

I have characterized my "Voyage of Discovery" as a journey into the unknown, just as Bugelski taught me that: "Science is the explication of the unknown." In so doing, I have likened my learning to the mountains of knowledge. I have climbed to acquire the basic tools that I needed (see Figure 19).

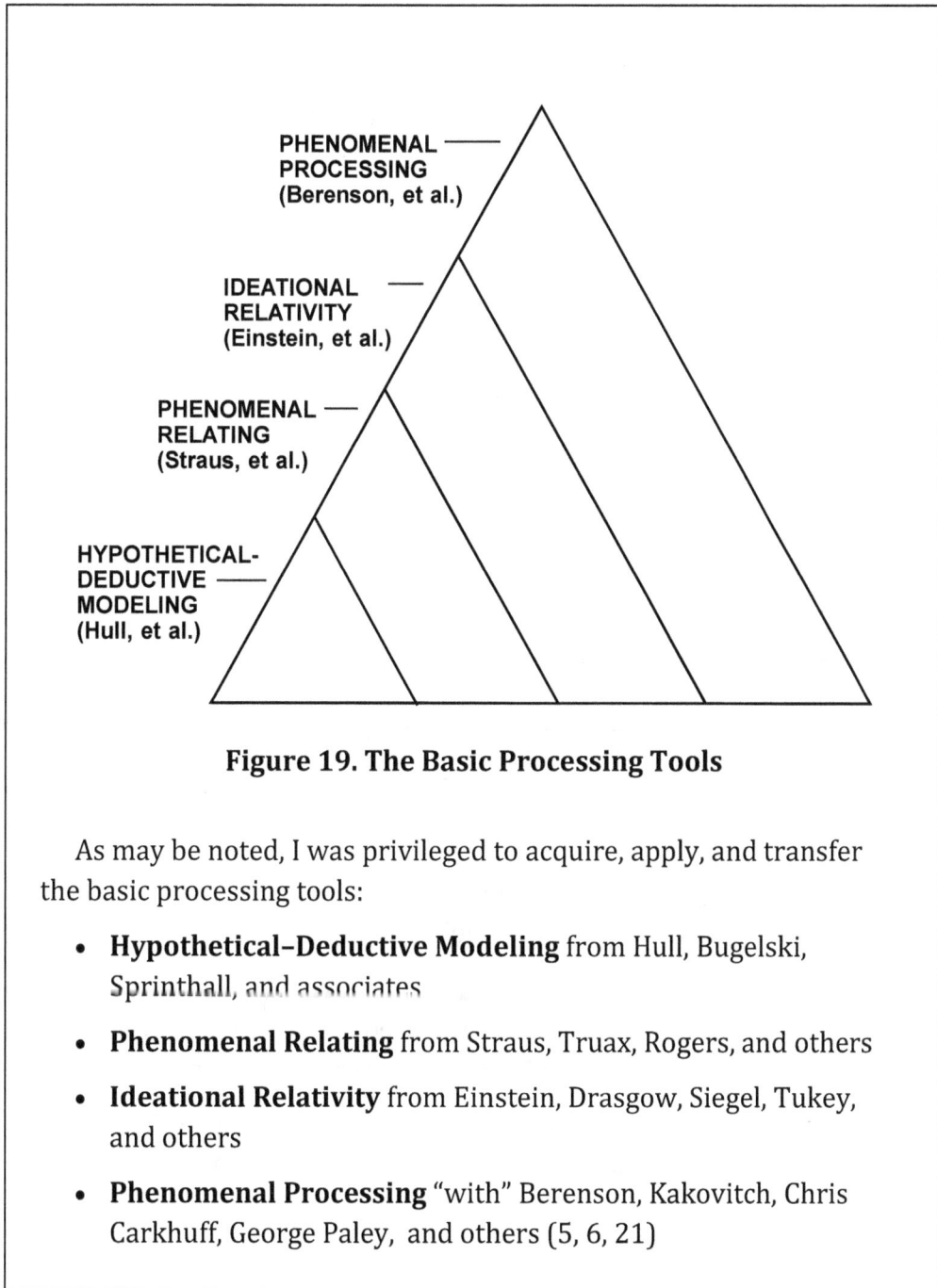

Figure 19. The Basic Processing Tools

As may be noted, I was privileged to acquire, apply, and transfer the basic processing tools:

- **Hypothetical–Deductive Modeling** from Hull, Bugelski, Sprinthall, and associates

- **Phenomenal Relating** from Straus, Truax, Rogers, and others

- **Ideational Relativity** from Einstein, Drasgow, Siegel, Tukey, and others

- **Phenomenal Processing** "with" Berenson, Kakovitch, Chris Carkhuff, George Paley, and others (5, 6, 21)

Human Endeavors

Climbing these mountains of knowledge and skills gave us the opportunity to address ourselves to all the areas of human endeavor (see Figure 20):

- The Mechanical Processing Systems based upon S–R Conditioned Responding that yield Mechanical Capital Development or mCD

- The Information Representing Systems based upon S–O–R Discriminative Learning that yield Information Capital Development or ICD

- The Human Processing Systems based upon S–P–R Generative Processing that yield Human Capital Development or HCD

- The Organizational Processing Systems based upon S–OP–R Organizational Processing that yield Organizational Capital Development or OCD

- The Marketplace Processing Systems based upon S–MP–R Marketplace Processing that yield Marketplace Capital Development or MCD

- The Community Processing Systems based upon S–CP–R Community Processing that yield Community Capital Development or CCD

- The Cultural Processing Systems based upon S–CP′–R Cultural Processing that yield Cultural Capital Development or CCD′

- The Economic Processing Systems based upon S–EP–R Economic Processing that yield Economic Capital Development or ECD

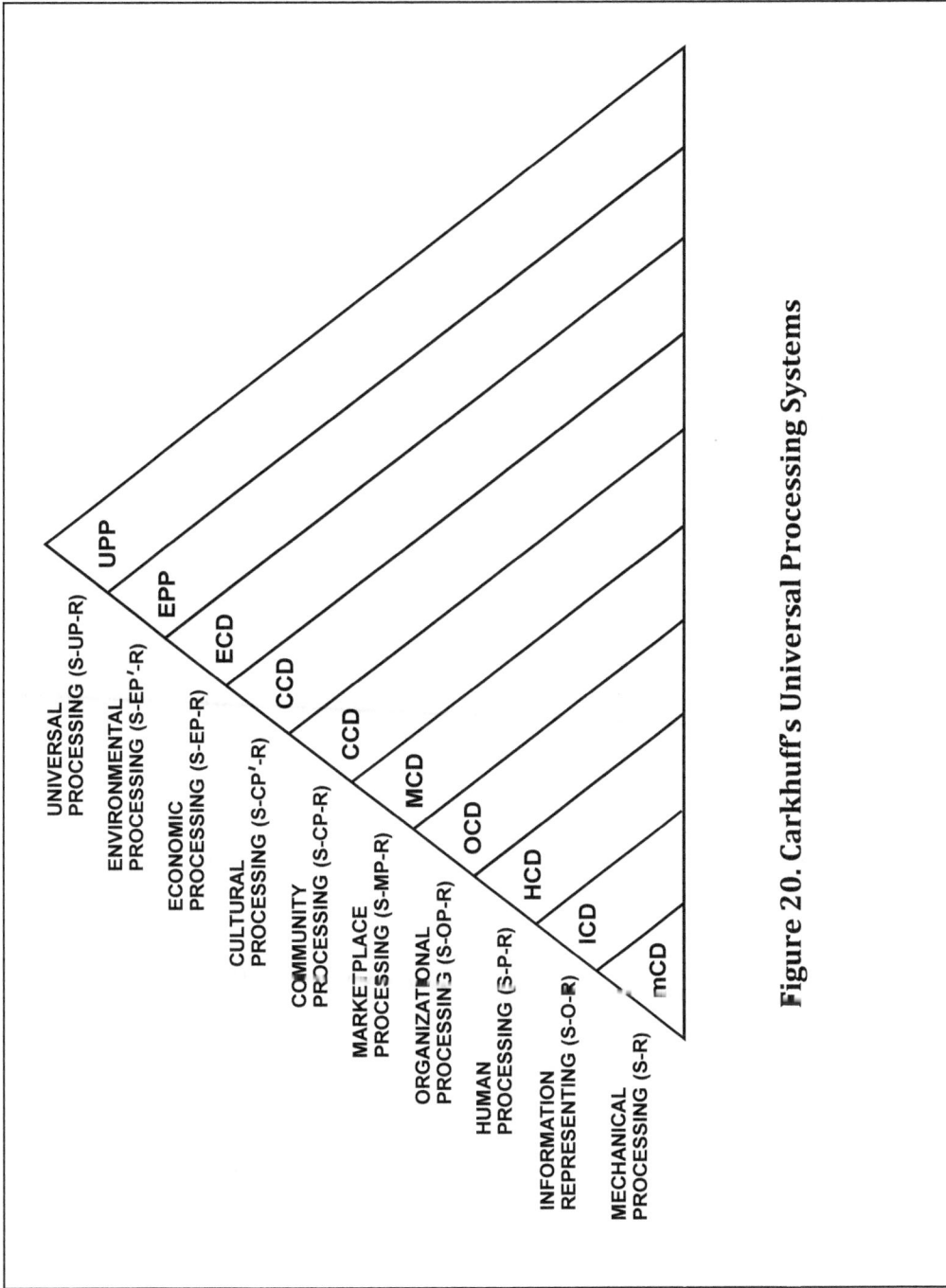

Figure 20. Carkhuff's Universal Processing Systems

UNIVERSAL PROCESSING (S-UP-R)

ENVIRONMENTAL PROCESSING (S-EP'-R)

ECONOMIC PROCESSING (S-EP-R)

CULTURAL PROCESSING (S-CP'-R)

COMMUNITY PROCESSING (S-CP-R)

MARKETPLACE PROCESSING (S-MP-R)

ORGANIZATIONAL PROCESSING (S-OP-R)

HUMAN PROCESSING (S-P-R)

INFORMATION REPRESENTING (S-O-R)

MECHANICAL PROCESSING (S-R)

UPP

EPP

ECD

CCD

CCD

MCD

OCD

HCD

ICD

mCD

To sum, the basic processing tools enable us to generate all forms of New Capital Development or **NCD: MCD, OCD, HCD, ICD, mCD.** Moreover, NCD empowered us to generate all forms of Community, Cultural, and Economic Capital Development **(CCD, CCD′, ECD).**

Currently, we are working with others to explicate the Environmental Processing Potential **(EPP)** of aligning with Environmental Processing Systems **(S–EP′–R):**

Conditions:	Under the requirements of asymmetrically curvilinear systems
Functions:	Interdependent life-cycle processing functions are discharged
Components:	By unequal multidimensional vectorial modeling components
Processes:	Enabled by generative processing systems
Standards:	To achieve continuously changing standards

Again, changeability is the key to this operational definition.

Our culminating mission is to operationally define **"The Universal Processing Potential" (UPP)** of **Universal Processing Systems (S–UP–R):**

Conditions:	Under higher-order phenomenal processing requirements
Functions:	All phenomena are genetically encoded to process interdependently
Components:	By multidimensional phenomena unequal in their processing power
Processes:	Empowered by interdependent generative processing systems
Standards:	To achieve continuously-changing phenomenal standards

In all of these instances, we can observe how higher-order phenomena generate the conditions for lower-order phenomena: **UPP > EPP > ECD > CCD' > CCD > MCD > OCD > HCD > ICD > mCD.** These conditions define the operations that are required of the lower-order phenomena.

Thus, for example, the conditions of the marketplace (**MCD**) define the requirements for the organization (**OCD**). Likewise, the conditions of the organization define the requirements for human performance (**HCD**).

So we need only to look up to the cascading conditions within which we are nested to discriminate the requirements to which we are dedicated. These are our inductive scientific efforts to build our hypothetical deductive models.

In all of these instances, we can also measure the levels of achievement in our standards by the hypotheses that we test with lower-order phenomena. Thus, for example, just as the standards of the marketplace (**MCD**) are measured by the achievements of the organization (**OCD**), so are the standards of the organization measured by the achievements of human performance (**HCD**).

So we need only to look down to the cascading standards to test the levels of achievement of our responses to hypothetical projections. These are the deductive technological tests of our hypotheses derived from our hypothetical deductive models.

This is precisely where Human Generativity is required in all Human Endeavors:

- Comparing the requirements of the conditions in which we are "housed" with our capacity-building potential

- Intentionally generating that place in our world in which we wish to live, learn, and work:

    – As Generators who create our own changeable destinies
    – As Innovators who improve our human capacities to meet conditional requirements
    – As Commercializers who create the prosperity that empowers our own participation and peace

In all of these processes, we followed the New Hypothetical–Deductive Modeling Protocols:

- Inductively building Hypothetical–Deductive Constructs to explain the unknown (**Science**)

- Deductively deriving the Testable Hypothesis to test the known (**Technologies**)

In so doing, we employed the Hypothetical–Deductive Modeling Processes:

- **Relating** to become "one" with the phenomena with successive approximations of accuracy of their processing systems

- **Representing** the phenomenal processing systems with special regard to their essential "unequality" and "relativity"

- **Reasoning** by expanding and narrowing the potentially differentiated processing systems employed by the phenomena in the different stages of their development

Clearly, our ultimate mission for "The Science of Science" is "The Universal Processing System." We continue to approach this moving target along with our colleagues.

RRC   January, 2011
The McLean Project   McLean, Virginia

In summary, Carkhuff eagerly embraces any human endeavors and problems encountered along the way. Along with his associates, he continues to generate the scientific "breakthroughs" and technological solutions.

Phenomenal Processing Freedom

Together, we have discovered Nature's Principles of Generativity: (1)

Generativity is a function of the processing between unequal phenomenal systems (real and/or virtual) and the degrees of freedom which each of these systems has to invest and process interdependently and synergistically (where each grows as the other grows).

In so doing, we have defined Phenomenal Processing Freedom: Those who are most marginal are prepared with the greatest degrees of freedom (variability) to relate interdependently and synergistically with diverse phenomena (unequality) and generate explosive new images of phenomena (changeability).

This contrasts vividly with constructs such as Statistical Process Control from an earlier stage of science. Those who are most defined by consensus (central tendencies) have the fewest degrees of freedom to relate to any phenomena except those most similar (equality) and, thus, dictate shrinking images of all phenomena (initially stasis, transitionally linearity, ultimately disappearance).

Phenomenal Processing Freedom defines the ingredients of The Science of Change!

The Possibilities Mind

The Possibilities Mind is both the subject of our work and its vehicle (1). Substance, meaning, and perspective, are all integrally related here. To have meaning, perspective must merge substance, the personal, and the creative. This merging can occur only with a view from the changing margins, beyond the borders. When the mind is ego-free, relating fully and merging with processing, changing phenomena, then elevated levels of meaning are clear and available. In these precious moments, phenomena demonstrate their empowerment and freedom; the mind—now The Possibilities Mind— grows more comfortable flirting with new universes.

Penetrating visions emerge from the adventure of reaching into how and why the unequal companions of Nature relate, process, and transform their interdependent social relationships—that is, how and why the phenomena are empowered to contribute to reinvention, even their own demise. The inclusive perspective embraces the generativity when changeability and freedom live and serve one another at the countless instants that asymmetrical, unfinished Time begins.

The function of The Possibilities Mind is thus to conjure up timeless perspectives. That mind is faithful to its possibilities function when relating in order to align; aligning in order to empower; empowering in order to free all processing phenomena.

On the changing margin, beyond the borders, The Possibilities Mind grasps a vision of Nature's reinventing community of unequal companions. It is here in this asymmetrical community of "leftovers" where the power of freedom is processed into the primal life force of change. It is here where the life force of change is processed into freedom.

By contrast, conditioned intellectual isolation, purity, and stasis yield but an incomplete skeleton of "probables." The heart and soul are gone; the mind and perspectives atrophy.

Whatever is asymmetrical, and therefore by definition unfinished, is alive with changing imperfections. Possibilities substance, art, science, philosophy, psychology, and, yes, possibilities perspectives are imperfect, asymmetrical, unfinished. They live. They are leftovers! Only leftovers are free!

Chapter 7
Human Generativity ——————

It is shameful that science itself takes so long to catch up with its own generators. Witness, Einstein: If not for World War II and J. Robert Oppenheimer's Manhattan Project, the public might not have known about Einstein's relativity!

Witness, Carkhuff: If not for the malaise of American civilization due to her people's fatuous consumption on our fourth "economic bubble," we might never be introduced to Carkhuff's generativity!

To understand Carkhuff, we must understand "The Pure Scientist." He dedicated years defining Science as Information-Representation: scaling the levels of conceptual, operational, dimensional, vectorial, and phenomenal information. Then in a few moments, he explodes the phenomenal level with Paradigmetric Measurement of all "field information" (think Einstein!): space, time, temperature, mass, charge.

In Jim Drasgow's terms:

Ideas take a long time in gestation, but only moments to birth.

In this context, there are many schools of thought that claim the tutelage of Carkhuff and influence upon his body of work. The truth is that some may be right! The truth is that Carkhuff is eclectic in his approach to *all* science.

In this review, I have attempted to make clear the influences that Carkhuff has revealed for as he says repeatedly, "None of us were born fully actualized!"

In this context, here are samples of Carkhuff's reactions:

- "I am most proud of Bugelski's claim for **The Hullian School of Behavioral Science.**"

- "I am most baffled by the claims of **The Rogerian School of Non-Directive Philosophy.**"

- "I am most committed to **The Einsteinian Orientation to The Ideational Sciences.**"

Behaviorism

In Carkhuff's exit interview from SUNY Buffalo with Dick Bugelski, Chair of Psychology, Bugelski said the following:

- "If you stay, you'll have waves of doctoral students to promote your work and you'll become the most famous scientist in history."

Carkhuff responded:

- "I'm most grateful for the powerful principles of Behaviorism under controlled conditions, but I have got to go out and find the principles of Behaviorism that operate under uncontrolled conditions."

Carkhuff accepted Dick Sprinthall's invitation to "save Springfield" and the rest, as they say, is history. A glorious history! Carkhuff made the most incredible demonstration of a "Community Turnaround" in the history of the world. He continues to apply his evolving models to socioeconomic demonstrations in communities and cultures around the world (8).

Phenomenalism

Carkhuff has made Phenomenalism a central ingredient of his Possibilities Science. But he did not discover these ingredients in his six-month visit with Carl Rogers at the University of Wisconsin Psychiatric Institute! Carkhuff's disappointment in Rogerian philosophy can be viewed most clearly in the recording of his exit interview (11).

RC:	"Dr. Rogers, you can open your position up and account for many if not most of the ingredients of therapeutic effectiveness."
CR:	"I'm not interested in opening the position up. The ingredients I have postulated are necessary and sufficient for therapeutic personality change."
RC:	"But Dr. Rogers, there are going to be many more ingredients added before we fill out the equation of therapeutic effectiveness."
CR:	"I am interested only in demonstrating the effectiveness of non-directive techniques with schizophrenic patients."
RC:	"But Dr. Rogers, training the clients in the dimensions that we have found to be effective would seem to be the most efficient and effective way to change people."
CR:	"I don't believe in training in empathy. Either you are born with it or not!"
RC:	"We have already demonstrated that we can train many different populations to be interchangeable in their empathic responses. They do so at levels higher than the **'expert'** therapists who have participated in your Psychotherapy Research Project."
CR:	"I am interested only in helping clients to achieve what they want."
RC:	"But Dr. Rogers, they want too little."

This excerpt illustrates Carkhuff's greatest problem with the **"Rogerians"**: they were theorists—not scientists. Their mission was to prove the efficacy of non-directive therapy with schizophrenic patients.

For Carkhuff, Rogers and his followers had excluded the most powerful source of learning—training! In hundreds of studies of training with all kinds of helpers—parents, teachers, and managers as well as counselors and therapists—Carkhuff established higher levels of interpersonal relating and resultant helpee outcomes than conventionally-educated helpers (11).

Moreover, Carkhuff established the pre-potency of "training as a preferred mode of treatment" for tens of thousands of helpees—children, students, workers, as well as clients and patients. Carkhuff established high levels of success in real-life indices of living, learning, and working outcomes (11).

Most conclusively, Carkhuff cites the hundreds of ex-offenders in the Springfield project who never offended again (8):

> **Against recidivism rates over 70%, we have demonstrated rates of 10% or less with all kinds of pathological populations.**

All helpers and helpees were products of systematic training in interpersonal-driven helping skills.

On the other hand, Carkhuff was a young Scientist-in-Training. Carkhuff had received a two-year NIH Post-Doctoral Research Fellowship to study "the common core of ingredients in all helping and human relationships." He studied all of the dominant therapeutic orientations of our time: psychodynamic, client-centered, behavioristic, trait-and-factor, existential.

Dutifully, Carkhuff analyzed all of the sessions of the different orientations and reported his conclusions:

1. All orientations to helping share a common core of relating skills centered around responding experientially and initiating experimentally (*The Sources of Gain in Counseling and Psychotherapy*, Holt, Rinehart and Winston, 1967).

2. The existing theoretical orientations are "Potential Preferred Modes of Treatment" which, under specifiable conditions (helpee characteristics), make unique contributions (*Beyond Counseling and Therapy,* Holt, Rinehart and Winston, 1967).

3. The same core of relating experiences also apply to all helping and human relationships for purposes of Human Resource Development, Education, and Rehabilitation: The effects of all potential treatment programs are contingent upon the levels of relating skills offered to the treated population (*Helping and Human Relations,* Holt, Rinehart and Winston, 1969).

It seemed to Carkhuff at the time that the **Psychodynamic** and **Nondirective** theoretical orientations were playing a zero-sum game in competition for the popular opinion of humanists: whatever the results of the hypothesis testing, they did *not* modify their theoretical orientations. This is common in all **Probability Science** where the theorists compete for the variability of a statically defined parametric marketplace.

As a lifelong scientist, Carkhuff understands the practitioners' lack of understanding of changeability as a super-ordinate construct of science: They did not comprehend the future of sciences.

Could it be that serious research into helping and human relating has regressed since Carkhuff moved on 50 years ago?!

In this context, it is important to emphasize that Carkhuff dedicated only five years (1963–1968) to his research on "victims" treated by traditional counseling and psychotherapy. It was in 1968 that he moved upstream to the community and socioeconomics to study where the bodies were being thrown in. It is left for Carkhuff to state his view of all of his scientific efforts:

To build inductively with phenomena and test deductively with hypothesis.

Fortunately, in Carkhuff's terms, "I went on to discover the ingredients of Phenomenalism in my studies with Straus, Truax, and Aspy." It has become central to Carkhuff's evolving Sciences of Possibilities and Generativity:

> **All science begins with the sensory experience of the scientist.** (11)

Ideation

Carkhuff was most influenced historically and is most committed futuristically to the **Ideational Sciences** of Einstein and others. Introduced to these bodies of works by Drasgow, he continues today in his work with Tom Kakovitch:

> **The most fundamental law of Nature is the conservation of information. While information can be generated, it cannot be destroyed. Einstein's** *"field equations"* **postulate mathematically the exchange of information between the fundamental forces of Nature and the** *"curved geometry of spacetime"* (21).

The most effective way to summarize Carkhuff's body of ideational work is in terms of his milestones in The Human Sciences (see Figure 21). As may be viewed, over the 50-year span of his scientific work, his Processing Systems have contributed a treasury of Capital Functions.

In so doing, he has merged with Nature to establish his generative leadership of The Human Sciences.

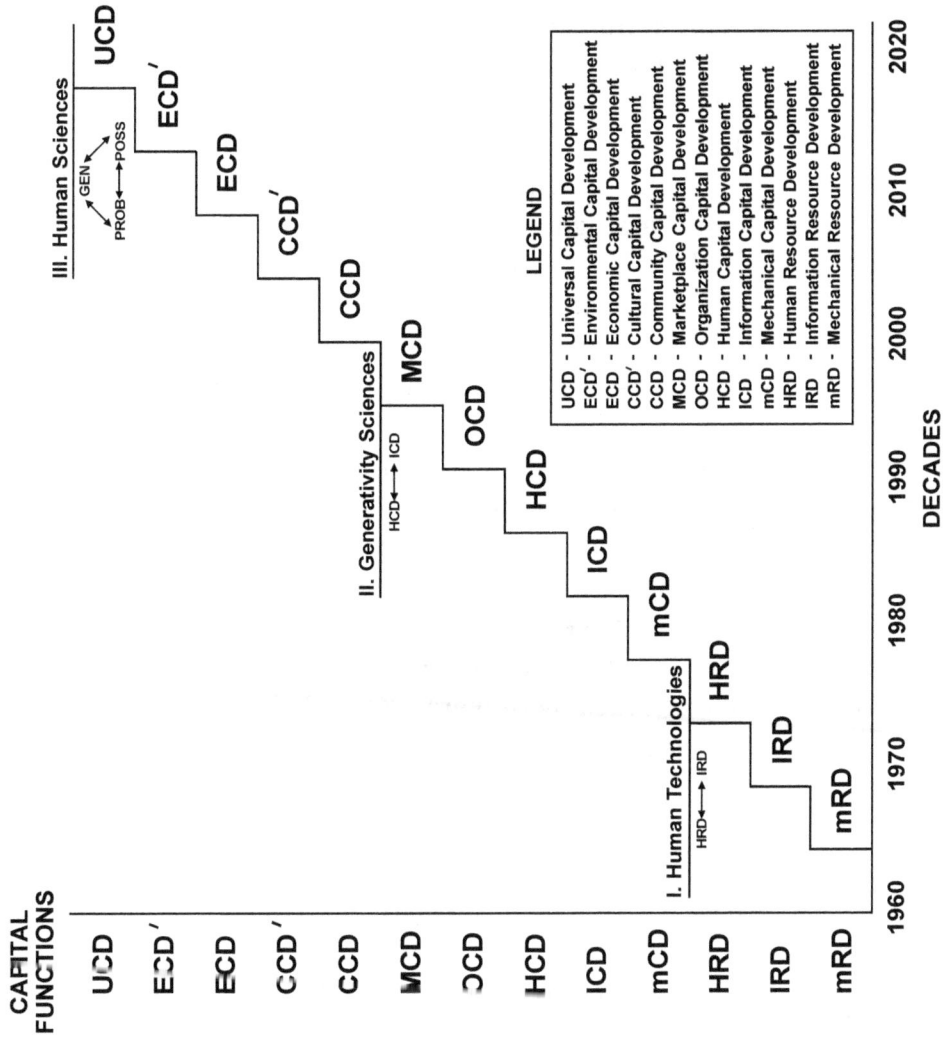

Figure 21. Milestones of Carkhuff's Human Sciences

Processing Potential

As may be noted in Table 4, Human Technologies **(HRD ↔ IRD)** are driven by Probabilities and Possibilities Sciences. In turn, Generativity Sciences are defined by synergistic Human and Information Capital Development **(HCD ↔ ICD).** Finally, Human Sciences are operationalized by the synergistic interaction of Probabilities, Possibilities, and Generative Sciences.

We may validate the Paradigm Shift to The Human Sciences with the Processing Systems and Capital Functions. As may be viewed, beginning inductively with the early Human Technologies (Phase I), every Processing System has been based upon S–R Conditioned Responding Systems. As may be noted, each level of processing is nested in higher-order processing systems.

In turn, beginning deductively with The Human Sciences (Phase III), each level of processing is nested in the superordinate Universal Processing System or UPS. Thus, UPS encodes all subordinate Processing Systems. All Processing Systems meet the criteria of Applied Science—operational, functional, replicable, measurable, developmental.

Beginning deductively with the Capital Functions, then, all Human Benefits are nested and encoded by Universal Capital: Environmental, Economic, Cultural, Community, Marketplace, Organization, Human, Information, Mechanical.

Table 4. The Processing Systems and Capital Functions of The Human Sciences

Scientific Phases	Processing Systems (Nested)	Capital Functions (Nested)
III. Human Sciences Gen ↗ ↘ Prob ⟷ Poss	S–**UPS**→R S–**EP′**→R	Universal Capital (**UC**) Environmental Capital (**EC′**)
	S–**EP**–R S–**CC′**–R S–**CC**–R	Economic Capital (**EC**) Cultural Capital (**CC′**) Community Capital (**CC**)
II. Generativity Sciences (**HCD** ⟷ **ICD**)	S–**MP**–R S–**OP**–R S–**HP**–R S–**IP**–R S–**mP**–R	Marketplace Capital (**MC**) Organization Capital (**OC**) Human Capital (**HC**) Information Capital (**IC**) Mechanical Capital (**mC**)
I. Possibilities Science (**HT** ⟷ **IT**)	S–**P**–R S–**O**–R S–R	Human Resource Development (**HRD**) Information Resource Development (**IRD**) Mechanical Resource Development (**mRD**)

Future Generativity

Empowered by The Human Sciences, Carkhuff has founded The McLean Project by integrating private and public sector initiatives dedicated to the generative leadership of a Free and Prosperous World (see Figure 22).

As may be viewed, the project generates solutions to the critical issues of the 21st century:

- **Terra Forma**—The global survival solutions to air, water, land, and sustainable food problems generated by "The Blue Revolution" that their work has created

- **Human Empowerment**—The individual and group solutions generated by Human, Information, and Mechanical Processing Technologies

- **Organization Optimization**—The organization solutions generated by "Real-Time Intelligence Resource Integration and Optimization"

- **Socioeconomic Growth**—The community, cultural, and economic solutions generated by Interdependent Cultural Relating, Electronic Participative Governance, and Entrepreneurial Economic Enterprise

Of course, all of these human solutions are integrated and elevated by the continuously growing "Science of Science":

- Probabilities Science and Parametric Measurement
- Possibilities Science and Non-Parametric Measurement
- Generativity Science and Paradigmetric Measurement

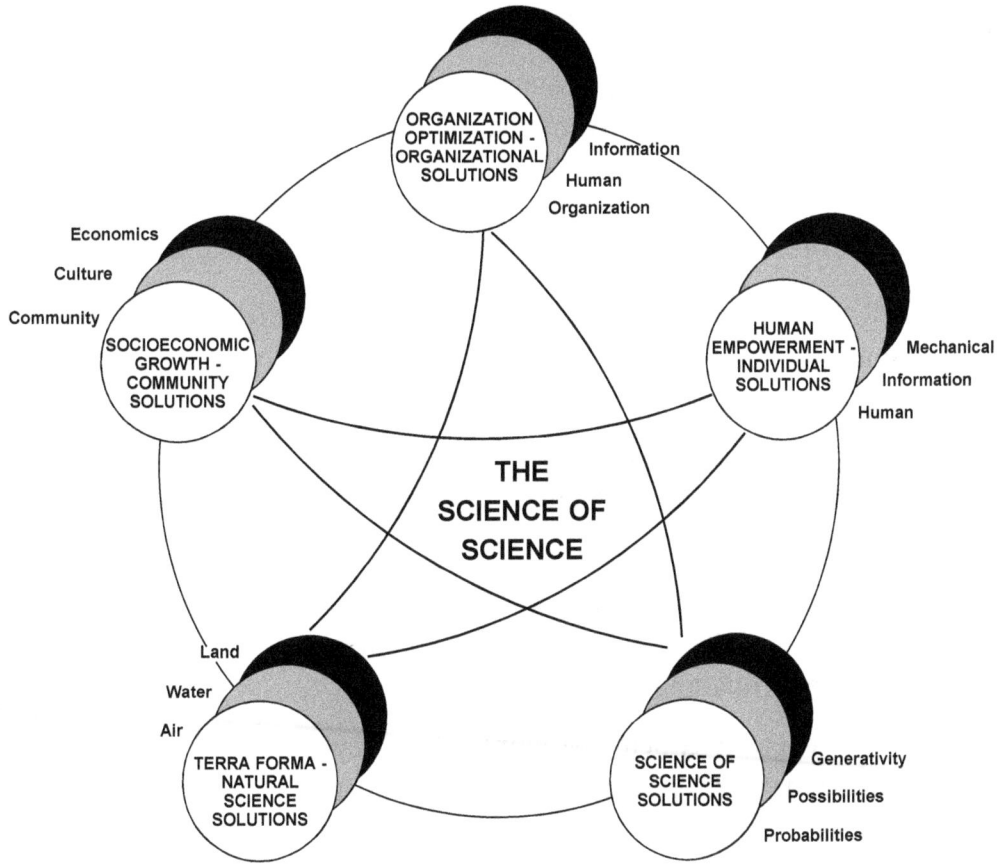

Figure 22. The McLean Project—"Science in the Service of Humankind"

Scientific Perspective

Perhaps the largest scientific perspective comes from Dick Sprinthall, a scholar in Probabilities Science and Parametric Measurement who taught Carkhuff Statistical Analysis more than 50 years ago. He has taken the full measure of Carkhuff's commitment to generating The Science of Science:

As a parametric scientist, I now stand in awe of The New Science that Carkhuff and his associates have discovered. Here are the salient features:

- It employs the full power of Probabilities Science and related Parametric Measurement to describe and predict all phenomena.

- It generates the full power of Possibilities Science and its Non-Parametric Measurements to relate, empower and free the full potential of all phenomena and, in so doing, directs the operations of Probabilities Science.

- The Generativity Sciences employ the prepotent power of Generative Processing—individual, organizational, community, cultural, economic and a new Paradigmetric Measurement System to represent the Universal Processing of all information.

A True Science—generative, measureable, and replicable! It explicates the unknown by describing, predicting, relating, empowering and releasing or freeing all phenomena (Sprinthall (8)).

The Changeability Standard

Carkhuff's central principle is changeability. Once again, changeability defines the standards by which we operationally define all phenomena:

Conditions:	Under asymmetrically curvilinear conditions
Functions:	interdependent life-cycle processing functions are discharged
Components:	by unequal multidimensional modeling components
Processes:	enabled by generative processing
Standards:	with changeability standards.

Changeability is thus the key to these operational definitions.

Whereas variability seeks to fix phenomena in a static state, changeability seeks to align with, first, naturalistic operations and, second, empowering interventionistic effects upon operations. Its view is inclusive, admitting variability as simply another instance of the changeable. Variability itself, though, is exclusive and eliminates all concepts of changeability.

These two contrasting principles shape the core of two very different sciences. Probabilities Science, which relies on variability, is highly artificial in origin, contributed by humankind's need to order and control its universe. This science fixes its data sources in two-dimensional matrices of rows and columns. It analyzes its data in statistics concerning the deviation of phenomena from derived central tendencies. In so doing, it loses much of the measuring of its original data through so-called "error variance." In this context, chaos and even relativity are misinterpretations.

Possibilities Science comes to us fashioned by observations of Nature herself. Nature speaks to us and tells us the following:

- All lower-order phenomena are genetically encoded by higher-order phenomena.

- All phenomena rotate to become drivers in processing (depending upon their purposes and ours).

Changeability is thus defined by all of these continuous operations:

- Phenomenal processing
- Inequality of processing
- Nested processing
- Genetic encoding of processing
- Rotating of processing systems

Together, these operations make up the Continuous Interdependent Processing Systems that define changeability. If we are continuously and interdependently processing, then we are continuously changing.

Changeability is the prepotent construct. It generates an infinite array of spiraling standards and serves as the driving function for variability. It empowers us to do *the right things,* while variability enables us to do *things right.* Again, we may even dedicate changeability to variability and the eternal task of narrowing variability around static standards.

In short, changeability is the engine of possibilities—the energy source of Nature's intelligence. It is a free seminal generator, certainly not something to be partitioned like variance. The artificiality of the latter may be employed to support a temporary fad-like commercial product or idea, or even scientific content; yet, all processing phenomena are ever, in truth, changeability companions.

As water springs from the special social relationship between hydrogen and oxygen, changeability springs from the unequal and social interdependent processing dynamics of Nature. As it is with Nature, so it is with The Possibilities Mind. Carkhuff is **The Possibilities Mind.** And both are unfinished!

In Transition

Summarizing my own work with Carkhuff, I would conclude the following:

- Carkhuff is **Pure Scientist,** pursuing the mission of Explicating the Unknown.

- Carkhuff is **Pure Generative Scientist** who in his lifetime has generated both the Sciences of Possibilities and Generativity to extend our existing Science of Probabilities.

- Carkhuff is **Pure Applied Scientist** whose current mission is as follows:

> **To create a New Paradigm for Science for an Elevated Platform for Civilization.**

Carkhuff continues to process interdependently with his processing partners in service of this mission. Pre-potent above all other processing, Carkhuff processes interdependently with the phenomena he is addressing.

Because he believes "Science is continuously and intentionally evolving," Carkhuff always concludes his Perspective Pieces with a Transition. So here goes:

In transition, Carkhuff's work reflects the core processes of Nature's Generativity:

> Carkhuff's contributions to **Universal Processing,** alone, qualify him for leadership among the greatest scientists of history. His nesting, encoding, and rotating of processing systems are the core processes of **Nature's Generativity.** In creating **The Human Sciences,** Carkhuff's bodies of work belong in **The Pantheon of Science** along with the works of DaVinci, Newton, and Einstein.

If all this sounds elegant, it is. Elegance is the ultimate test of all science. Carkhuff's work is the height of elegance. It is the ultimate and ubiquitous paradigm shift to the human being!

To sum, **The Human Sciences** culminates in **Human Generativity.** And Carkhuff is the father of them all.

Bernard G. Berenson, Ph.D.   January 1, 2010
                                                              Amherst, Massachusetts

References ━━━━━━━━━━━━━━━━

1. Berenson, B. G. *The Possibilities Mind.* Amherst, MA: HRD Press, 2001.

2. Berenson, B. G. and Cannon, J. R. *The Science of Freedom.* McLean, VA: American Noble Prize, 2006.

3. Bugelski, B. R. *Psychology of Learning.* New York: Holt, Rinehart, & Winston, 1956.

4. Bugelski, B. R. *Principles of Learning.* New York: Praeger, 1979.

5. Carkhuff, C. J. and Paley, G. *IONN—Interdependent Object Networking and Navigation System.* McLean, VA: GenStar, 2011.

6. Carkhuff, C. J. and Paley, G. *VOR—Virtual Organization Reality.* McLean, VA: GenStar, 2011.

7. Carkhuff, R. R. *Helping and Human Relations.* New York: Holt, Rinehart, & Winston, 1969.

8. Carkhuff, R. R. *Saving America: The Generativity Solution.* Amherst, MA: HRD Press, 2010.

9. Carkhuff, R. R. *The Human Sciences.* McLean, VA: The McLean Project, 2011.

10. Carkhuff, R. R. *The McLean Project.* McLean, VA: The McLean Project, 2011.

11. Carkhuff, R. R. and Berenson, B. G. *The New Science of Possibilities.* Amherst, MA: HRD Press, 2000,

12. Drasgow, J. Eclipsing All Great Works. Foreword, *The Freedom Wars.* Amherst, MA: HRD Press, 2004.

13. Einstein, A. *Relativity: The Special and General Theory.* New York: Henry Holt, 1931.

14. Einstein, A. *The Evolution of Physics.* Cambridge: University of Cambridge, 1938.

15. Einstein, A. *Collected Papers of Albert Einstein.* Princeton, NJ: Princeton University Press, 1989.

16. Garfield, E. *The 100 Books Most Cited by Social Scientists.* Philadelphia, PA: Number 37, Institute for Scientific Information, 1978(a).

17. Garfield, E. *The 100 Books Most Cited by Social Scientists.* Philadelphia, PA: Number 45, Institute for Scientific Information, 1978(b).

18. Hull, C. L. *Mathematics—Deductive Theory of Rote Learning.* New York: Appleton-Century-Crofts, 1940.

19. Hull, C. L. *Principles of Behavior.* New York: Appleton-Century-Crofts, 1943.

20. Hull, C. L. *A Behavior System.* New Haven, CT: Yale University Press, 1952.

21. Kakovitch, T. *The Fifth Force.* McLean, VA: The McLean Project, 2012.

22. Pavlov, I. P. *Conditioned Reflexes.* Oxford: Oxford University Press, 1927.

23. Rogers, C. R. *Client-Centered Therapy.* Boston, MA: Houghton Mifflin, 1951.

24. Rogers, C. R. The Necessary and Sufficient Conditions of Therapeutic Personality Change. *Journal of Consulting Psychology,* 1957, *22*, 95–103.

25. Rogers, C. R., E. T. Gendlin, D. Kiesler, and C. B. Truax. *The Therapeutic Relationship and Its Impact.* Madison, WI: University of Wisconsin Press, 1967.

26. Siegel, S. and Tukey, J. *Nonparametric Statistics for the Behavioral Sciences.* Washington, DC: American Association for the Advancement of Science, 1959.

27. Sprinthall, R. C. *Basic Statistical Analysis.* Boston, MA: Allyn and Bacon, 2011.

28. Sprinthall, R. C. *SPSS.* Boston, MA: Pearson Education, Inc. 2009.

29. Straus, E. *Phenomenology: Pure and Applied.* Pittsburgh: Duquesne University Press, 1964.

30. Truax, C. B. and Carkhuff, R. R. *Toward Effective Counseling and Therapy.* Chicago: Aldine, 1967.

31. Watson, J. *Behaviorism.* Chicago: University of Chicago Press, 1930.

32. Whitaker, C. The Technique of Family Therapy. In G. P. Shovelet, *Changing Sexual Values and the Family.* Springfield, IL: Charles Thomas, 1976.

Selected Einstein References ━━━

Einstein, Albert. 1916. *Relativity: The Special and the General Theory.* London: Methuen, 1920.

Einstein, Albert. 1922a. *The Meaning of Relativity.* Princeton: Princeton University Press, 1922.

Einstein, Albert. *Sidelights on Relativity.* New York: Dutton, 1922.

Einstein, Albert. *Essays in Science.* New York: Philosophical Library, 1934.

Einstein, Albert. *The World As I See It.* New York: Philosophical Library, 1949.

Einstein, Albert. *Out of My Later Years.* New York: Philosophical Library, 1950.

Einstein, Albert. *Einstein on Humanism.* New York: Philosophical Library, 1950.

Einstein, Albert. *Ideas and Opinions.* New York: Random House, 1954.

Einstein, Albert, and Leopold Infeld. *The Evolution of Physics: The Growth of Ideas from Early Concepts to Relativity and Quanta.* New York: Simon & Schuster, 1938.

Einstein, Elizabeth Roboz. *Hans Albert Einstein: Reminiscences of His Life and Our Life Together.* Iowa City: University of Iowa Press, 1991.

Isaacson, W. *Einstein: His Life and Universe.* New York: Simon and Schuster, 2007.

UNIVERSAL
PROCESSING (S-UP-R)

ENVIRONMENTAL
PROCESSING (S-EP'-R)   UPP

ECONOMIC
PROCESSING (S-EP-R)   EPP

CULTURAL
PROCESSING (S-CP'-R)   ECD

COMMUNITY
PROCESSING (S-CP-R)   CCD

MARKETPLACE
PROCESSING (S-MP-R)   CCD

ORGANIZATIONAL
PROCESSING (S-OP-R)   MCD

HUMAN
PROCESSING (S-P-R)   OCD

INFORMATION
REPRESENTING (S-O-R)   HCD

MECHANICAL   ICD
PROCESSING (S-R)   mCD

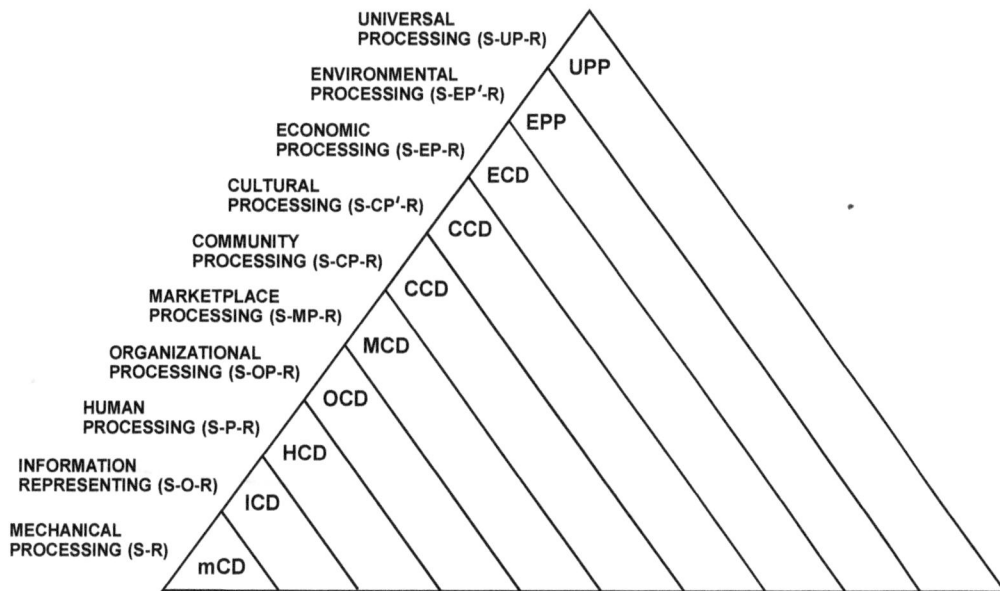

Carkhuff's Universal Processing Systems

www.ingramcontent.com/pod-product-compliance
Lightning Source LLC
Chambersburg PA
CBHW062107090426
42741CB00015B/3348